evolved girl™
How to Transform and Live Your Best Life
2nd Edition

Dr. Jacqueline Deas

Published by
Evolved You, LLC
Columbia, SC
evolvedyou.net

Copyright © 2023, 2016 by Jacqueline Deas

All rights reserved. Reproduction of this book in any manner, in whole or part, without written permission of the publisher is prohibited. Specific requests may be sent to the following email address: evolvedgirl@evolvedyou.net.

First paperback edition 2016.

Some of the names in this book have been changed to protect the privacy of individuals involved.

Library of Congress Cataloging-in-Publication Data

on file at the Library of Congress

This book is not intended to replace the advice of or treatment by other healthcare professionals. It should be considered an additional resource only. Questions and concerns about mental or physical health should always be discussed with a doctor or other healthcare professional. Neither the publisher nor the author shall be held liable or responsible for any loss or damage allegedly arising from any suggestion or information contained in this book.

Praise from Students Who Read Evolved Girl

- I made the "A" Honor Roll. I am the first one in my family to make the honor roll.
- I was angry. At home, we argued about everything. I am different at home. I'm working things out at home. We don't argue as much. I am listening more.
- I brought my grades up. I made the AB Honor Roll for the first time. I set goals for myself to do better in school.
- I am more confident and I feel better about myself.
- I was a C/D student. I now make A's and B's. I set goals to learn.
- My relationships have improved. I am more friendly and I have better grades. *(Other students confirmed that she is friendlier).*
- I am doing better with being on time. My math grade has improved.
- I was getting some bad grades. I have improved in math, science, and social studies because I study more. I created new goals.
- I bought a new planner and put my activities and assignments in it. I am more focused. I went up in all my grades except social studies.
- I am learning how to handle conflicts. I don't have as much conflict.
- I can speak up for myself now.
- I believe that I can be a success story even if people in my family aren't.

Praise from Teachers (of Evolved Girls)

- Student does not use profanity in PE anymore! I recently found out that she was in the Evolved Girl group. (From the PE teacher)
- Student participates and talks in class now. Prior to joining Evolved Girl, she did not really talk in class–at all. Now she talks.
- Student is not messy like she used to be! She is more mindful of how she acts and how it affects others.
- There is a new student in class that many of the students don't like because she whines and cries a lot. Two girls (Evolved Girls) embraced her and took her under their wings. They have become protective of her. Before joining the group, I'm not sure they would have done that.
- Student takes learning more seriously. She is more focused and her grades improved from C and D's to B's.
- Student is showing confidence in herself.

Hey Evolved Girl!

Welcome to the Evolved Girl family! We're here to help you become the best version of yourself. This book features stories of girls who have transformed and are eager to assist you with your own metamorphosis.

As a school counselor, I have worked with elementary, middle, and high school students in various settings. I have also served as an administrator and instructor at universities. I'm grateful for the opportunity to have visited schools in Africa and Europe. These experiences have given me a better understanding of students and the different stages of their development.

Though I am now a professional adult, I share something in common with you—I was once a girl, too. I wish there had been an Evolved Girl book or program to guide me during my school years. I grew up in a loving family, yet I faced some challenges alone because I did not fully understand my own worth or how to use my voice. Through this book, I aim to impart wisdom from my roles as an educator and counselor, while also speaking from the heart of the girl I once was.

My goal is to inspire you and help you understand your value and power. Just like a butterfly, you have the wings to reach new heights! Let's go on this journey together!

To Your Evolution,
Dr. Jacqueline Deas

Dedication

This book is dedicated to the beautiful girls who played a part in building this program and committing to their own growth. You inspired me to evolve! You learned a lot from me, but I learned more from you. I am a better leader, counselor, and coach because of you. You taught me how to have fun, dream in full color, and how to tap into my creativity and purpose in a bigger way. Thank you for taking me along on your journey! I love you girls!

TABLE OF CONTENTS

Acknowledgments	8
About Evolved Girl	11
Chapter 1: Butterfly Magic – Preparing For Your Metamorphosis	20
Chapter 2: Wings Of Influence How To Unleash The Leader In You	28
Chapter 3: Butterfly Brain Power – Secrets To School Success	38
Chapter 4: Dream Big And Fly High – The Guide To Achieving Your Goals	55
Chapter 5: Worthy Wings – Embracing Your Value	71
Chapter 6: Butterfly Charm – Winning With Habits, Attitude, And Manners	81
Chapter 7: Butterfly Harmony – Handling Friendships, Girl Drama, And Bullying	94
Chapter 8: Unfold Your Future Wings – Exploring Careers	109
Chapter 9: Brave Wings – Standing Tall Against Peer Pressure	122
Chapter 10: Love Your Wings – A Journey To Self-Care	128
Chapter 11: Measure Your Wingspan – Evaluating Your Journey	145
Chapter 12: Become A Metamorphosis Mentor – Inspire Change In Others	150

Acknowledgments

There are many wonderful people to thank for the Evolved Girl movement. This was too big a job to do alone, and I am thankful for the love and support from so many.

Melissa Royalty, thank you for allowing me to create the Evolved Girl program at Pine Tree Hill Elementary. You are an awesome leader and educator! JaaDaa Holcombe, thank you for the opportunity to empower girls at Whitley Elementary. You are an outstanding principal!

Ramani, our Evolved Girl Ambassador, you have truly transformed! Thank you for sharing wisdom with the girls. You inspire them in a big way!

My husband, John, you always support my professional and personal goals. You give me the space to evolve and create. You are a significant contributor to my evolution! I love you!

To my KBA Coaches: Frazelma, Chonta, Ladean, and Darnell—you helped me transform Evolved Girl! This wouldn't have been possible without your expertise. Thank you for working with me and guiding me on my journey!

The Evolved Girl Book Review Team consisted of a group of awesome educators, parents, and youth advocates including: Angela Armwood, Dr. Jamie Bates, Alicia Escalante-Tyler (along with Girl Scouts of West Central Florida Troop 33107), Michelle Elmore, Mayumi Escalante, Walter Freeman, Linda Horton, Audra Kirkwood (an advisor to the Evolved Girl program), Frazelma Lynn, Michelle Murray, Melissa Royalty, Myra Slayton, Dr. Theresa Spiller, Donna Slack-Outen, Della

Robinson, and Karisma Zender. You played a big part in helping me deliver a quality book to our girls!

Evolved Girl Student Contributors: Ramani, Mani, Anyielle, and Mallory. Thank you for your contribution to Evolved Girl! Your work and commitment will inspire and empower girls all over the world. I appreciate you more than you know. Keep up the good work, and remember your stories and who you are!

Special thanks to the Evolved Girl Branding Team, composed of girls from elementary, middle, and high schools, including Ramani, Sofie, Lina, Mani, and Anyielle. Your invaluable contributions were significant in guiding and supporting our branding efforts.

Mrs. Greta Hunt (My sister who is also a School Counselor): Thanks for supporting me and Evolved Girl. I appreciate your contribution.

Mrs. Cassandra East (Reading Intervention Coach, mother, and wife): Thanks for teaching girls about the power of reading. I've watched you do your magic with students as it relates to reading. You are certainly an awesome and effective Reading Coach.

Ms. Bell, Math Intervention Coach (Math Intervention Coach): Thanks for sharing tips with the girls about math! You have a way of shaping their minds and making it easy for them to learn math.

Shastra Solomon, M.D., thanks for your support and encouragement to the girls! You are not the ordinary doctor. Your words of wisdom and care continue to guide students to better health. Nurse Tameka Bolden, thanks for teaching the girls about self-care and self-love. You are an awesome school nurse!

To my Zeta Phi Beta family, thanks for your never-ending support and sisterhood!

Parents, thanks for allowing your daughters to share their experiences and help other girls evolve.

To my big Evolved Girls, Destiny Harris and Nia Kirkwood. I'm so proud of you. Thanks for allowing me to be a part of your journey. More important, thanks for all that you bring to my life.

ABOUT EVOLVED GIRL

Evolved Girl is a movement, program, and book designed for school-aged girls like you. It began in 2016 at Pine Tree Hill Elementary School in Camden, South Carolina. This book serves as a toolkit to assist you with grades, friendships, peer pressure, girl drama, self-esteem, emotional well-being, and managing conflicts with others. Evolved Girl aims to help you achieve success in every area of your life.

You might wonder why we chose the name *Evolved Girl*. *Evolve* means to change or transform. Our symbol for Evolved Girl is the butterfly. Butterflies evolve from a caterpillar through the process of metamorphosis. But, butterflies aren't the only ones who transform!

About Evolved Girl

Here's how Evolved Girl began. Once upon a time, I went into a 5th-grade class to provide a classroom guidance lesson. (The lessons I taught were about life skills, friendships, managing behavior, character, career awareness, and other topics.) While teaching, a student remarked, "Why don't we have a girls' group? Groups exist for the kids that make bad choices. They get rewards and snacks for having good behavior and doing what we already do. We fall between the cracks because we do the right things. Everybody knows the names of the bad kids." Another girl chimed in, "What about us, Mrs. Deas? What about us leaders who want to grow and be our best?"

At that moment, their words tugged at my heart. I felt their concern. The girls urged me to do something I had never considered before. No students had ever convinced me to start a group quite like these girls did. As they spoke and expressed their concerns about bullying, grades, low self-esteem, family problems, and issues with both girls and boys, they connected with the little girl I once was. I promised them I would start a group.

The question *"What about us?"* stayed in my mind all day. It followed me to sleep, and I tossed and turned that night. I remembered a statement my mentor said, "If it's in your power to change and improve something, do it." I went to my principal, Mrs. Royalty, and talked to her about the girls' group. She said, "Sounds like a good idea. Do it!" The Evolved Girl group and book were born! I then created forms and processes to track data to see if the program helped the girls. This book addresses the *"What about"* questions and topics from girls.

WHAT ABOUT?

- Grades
- Girl drama and and conflict
- Attitude, mindset, and manners
- Bullying
- Getting along with teachers I don't like or trying to make a good impression.
- Social media
- Preparing for college, career, or work
- Peer pressure
- My emotions, anxiety and depression
- Self-esteem and confidence
- Family conflict
- Handling change

Discoveries About Evolved Girl

I did what the girls asked; we began the group meetings. The girls enjoyed hot chocolate, donuts, and their favorite snacks during the group meetings. They chatted, shared, and prepared for their metamorphoses. After meeting for 10 weeks, the girls had noticeable changes that were confirmed by teachers, administrators, and parents! They experienced and created a Butterfly Effect, and the rest is history! History is still being made, thanks to girls like you.

About Evolved Girl

First Evolved Girls. (Two groups combined)

Evolved Girls in Texas   Evolved Girls in Alabama

The Butterfly Effect

When a small change has a big impact, we call it the Butterfly Effect. Meteorologist Edward Lorenz developed this concept. Here's an example of the Butterfly Effect: Two fifth-grade girls talked with me about starting a girls' group. That quick conversation and request led to the creation of the Evolved Girl program and book, which now inspires girls in the U.S. and around the world.

When the Evolved Girls completed their evaluations at the end of the group, we discovered that the impact was huge. Later, more evaluations came from students and teachers across several states. Data from the program proved the following:

- Grades improved and many students made honor roll for the first time
- Students learned about leadership and became role models
- Girls learned how to handle conflicts at school and home
- Emotional well-being improved (less anxiety and depression)
- Confidence grew
- Girls understood and appreciated their value
- Girls became more compassionate and empathetic toward other students
- Girls understood their superpowers and strengths

About Evolved Girl

What Will the Evolved Girl Experience Do For You?

You might wonder, "How will the Evolved Girl book and experience help me? What can I expect?" The goal is to help you and girls throughout the world:

- ✓ Understand how to stand out as a leader;
- ✓ Build your confidence so that you are powerful and unstoppable;
- ✓ Create the mindset, attitude, and manners so people never forget you;
- ✓ Achieve academic success so that you feel good about your grades;
- ✓ Discover your superpower and make the best decisions for your future;
- ✓ Learn the secret to making your dreams come true;
- ✓ Handle peer pressure and drama so you can feel peace at home and school;
- ✓ Manage your behavior so that others don't have to try to control you;
- ✓ Improve your emotional, physical, and mental well-being so that you keep your "happy" or get it back; and
- ✓ Use your voice to protect and empower yourself.

These skills are important because mastering them now can save you heartache and time later. The life skills you will learn are the same ones many adults are still trying to master. You have a head start!

*Keep a dictionary close. You may notice words in this book that you don't know. Don't get nervous. It's on purpose! ☺ These words are here to build your vocabulary.

The Evolved Girl Pledge

A pledge is a promise. The Evolved Girl pledge reminds you of who you are. Each Evolved Girl group starts with this pledge. Be sure to memorize it and say it daily.

evolved girl pledge

I am designed for success.
I make a positive difference in my school, family and community.
I see the best in myself and others.
I choose to make good choices.
I am a responsible leader and visionary with integrity and purpose.

Your Introduction to Butterfly Cathy and Coach

Please welcome Cathy and Coach on this journey with you. Cathy is on the same journey as you. As she transforms from a caterpillar to a butterfly, you'll discover that you, too, are changing. Coach is the mentor who helps Cathy evolve.

CATERPILLAR CATHY **BUTTERFLY CATHY** **COACH**

About Evolved Girl

Evolved Girl Resources for You

Evolved Girl provides additional resources for your growth and fun at evolvedyou.net.

KINDLE: Evolved Girl is like your new BFF and go-to guide. It is also available on Kindle, where it was a #1- Amazon bestseller!

JOURNAL: Unlock the power of self-expression and personal reflection with the Evolved Girl Journal. Capture your emotions, thoughts, achievements, and the things you are thankful for in one space.

PLANNER: This planner is not just about organizing dates; it inspires action, goal-setting, and self-discovery. With dedicated spaces for important dates, to-do lists, and action plans, this planner is a roadmap for your transformation.

COLORING BOOK: Take a colorful and magical journey to self-care, good health, and good vibes. It's not just a coloring book; it's a path to peace, relaxation, and happiness as you take each stroke.

EVOLVED GIRL EMPOWERMENT PROGRAM: This program positions girls to thrive and soar academically, socially, and emotionally. Data from the program confirmed the transformation that girls experienced. Visit www.evolvedyou.net to learn how you can participate online or bring the program to your school or organization.

CHAPTER 1: BUTTERFLY MAGIC — Preparing for Your Metamorphosis

Once upon a time, a group of caterpillars met every day to play on the tree branches. They often raced to see who could crawl the fastest. Many loved the comfort of where they lived, but Caterpillar Cathy had a feeling that her current life was short.

One day, Cathy told the other caterpillars, "I had a dream that I was flying and had so much fun. I saw new places and did things I can't do now." The caterpillars laughed until their little stomachs ached. "Ha! Ha! That really was a dream! Caterpillars can't fly. We don't have wings!" they said with sarcasm. The other caterpillars whispered, "I guess she doesn't want to be like us anymore." Caterpillar Cathy told her friends, "I know that caterpillars don't fly. I wasn't a caterpillar in the dream. I'm sorry I shared my dream with you."

Chapter 1: Butterfly Magic

When Caterpillar Cathy fell asleep this time, she dreamed she had beautiful orange and red wings. She then spoke with another caterpillar with wings who said gently, "Cathy, you already have these wings inside you. To become a caterpillar with wings, you must travel a new path. The path you are on now won't lead you to your dream. If you don't make a move now, you may never fly. If not now, when?" Cathy awakened from her dream with a sense of urgency and excitement. It was time to travel a new path so she could evolve and live her best life.

About Evolved Girl

Would you believe that you have a lot in common with butterflies? Before a caterpillar becomes a butterfly, it experiences four stages: egg, caterpillar, pupa, and adult (the butterfly life).

In the first stage, an **egg** is hatched on a host plant. Next comes the **caterpillar stage**, a phase almost every kid has experienced with the slow, graceful caterpillar. The caterpillar sheds its skin several times. In your caterpillar stage, you won't shed skin. However, you will be encouraged to shed old ways of thinking, habits, and behaviors that may stop you from growing wings.

The grown caterpillar will leave the plant that fed it, similar to the way that babies quit drinking baby milk and move to solid foods. When the caterpillar sheds its skin for the last time, it becomes a **pupa**. This is the stage where metamorphosis begins. During metamorphosis, the caterpillar spins a silky, small knob that forms a protective covering or cocoon. Inside the cocoon, the caterpillar transforms into a butterfly. When the cocoon opens, the **butterfly** is ready to spread its wings and fly. The caterpillar has everything it needs to transform into a soaring butterfly.

Chapter 1: Butterfly Magic

Sometimes, butterflies stay close to the ground. When butterflies fly low, scientists call this *gully bottoming*. Examples of gully bottoming are settling for low grades, telling your business on social media, and gossiping. Don't swarm in low points. Instead, fly high like a butterfly.

Taylor's Story (real-life situation)

Taylor felt as if everything was going wrong. She was dealing with girl drama at school, low grades, and conflicts at home with her family. She came to my office in tears, saying she was depressed because her life felt out of control. She felt like a caterpillar crawling through life. I asked her a magical question, "If you could change your life, what would be different?" After some thought, a light bulb came on. She realized she could change her story by taking responsibility for her own success and failures. She worked to change her thoughts, behavior, and view of herself. Her results were significant: good friends, respect from others, the courage to stand up for herself, improved grades, and peace at home. She no longer dwelled in low places! She stopped whining and complaining. Taylor became the student others sought out for advice. Both the principal and assistant principal were amazed at her transformation!

About Evolved Girl

How Will You Transform?

If you had a conversation with a caterpillar, it might say, "Get a good look at me because you won't recognize me a month from now. Now you see me, soon you won't. I will look different, act different, and even soar! Even though I am crawling now, I will fly later. If other caterpillars can transform into butterflies, why then, oh why, can't I?" If Taylor can transform, so can you!

Where would you like to see change in your life? Here are some areas where students set goals for change:

- Grades
- Relationships with teachers
- Conflict
- Behavior
- Health
- Negative thoughts
- Friendships
- Family relationships
- Perception of yourself

1. Write the areas that you want to change.

_____

_____

_____

_____

2. What do you have in common with caterpillars and butterflies?

_____

_____

_____

_____

Your Metamorphosis Tool Kit

As you embark on a new journey, you can view yourself as either a caterpillar or a butterfly. The caterpillar crawls, stays close to the ground, views the world from a small or limited perspective, and sees itself as a victim with no control. On the other hand, the butterfly sees itself as capable of flying high and creating change. Like Cathy, I believe you are ready to take off!

Have you ever seen hikers climbing a mountain? Or have you noticed that travelers carry luggage or backpacks with items they need for their journey? When you start your metamorphosis journey, you will need a few things in your backpack:

- Commitment to success (this means saying "yes" to success in your grades, behavior, friendships, and manners);

- Action and willingness to take the necessary steps for change;

- Focus and vision (the ability to concentrate on your success and see yourself as a winner);

- Confidence in yourself;

- Acceptance of yourself, your talents, intelligence, and uniqueness; and

- A winning attitude and mindset.

Remember this...

You have the power to change your life! There are wings inside you to help you soar to your full potential. You are going to use your wings to do incredible things. You are loved! Please feel my admiration and love for you as you read the pages of this book. You have a purpose, even if you don't yet understand it. I believe in you.

Chapter 1: Butterfly Magic

Take Your Parents on a Metamorphosis Journey With You

As you are preparing for your metamorphosis, you can help your parents start a new journey as well. Do you ever wish that your parents understood you better? Do you want them to know "how" to connect with you? Do you wish you could give them a small dose of guidance so that your relationship with them could be happier, more exciting, and peaceful?

I prepared a checklist that you can share with your parents. It is designed to help you and your parents connect and create a fun, happy, and strong relationship. The tips in this checklist come from the guidance and conversations with girls just like you.

The checklist, _10 Ways to Build a Dynamic Relationship With Your Daughter,"_ is free. Ask your parents (mom, dad, guardian, grandparents) to download with the QR code or link below.

www.evolvedyou.net/checklist-for-daughters

CHAPTER 2: WINGS OF INFLUENCE How to Unleash the Leader in You

When Cathy's friends saw her the next day, her behavior was different. "Must have had a dream about flying again, huh?" said one caterpillar. "Yep," replied Cathy. "Caterpillars don't fly; they crawl," remarked another caterpillar. She wondered if she would ever become the caterpillar she saw in the dream. She looked at herself but did not see any wings. Although she had never met a caterpillar with wings, she welcomed the idea of having wings and often visualized herself flying.

Cathy fell asleep again. In her dream, a Messenger said, "If you want to fly, cease your caterpillar thoughts and habits. The caterpillar will soon die, and your name will change to Butterfly Cathy." When she awakened, something was different. Cathy tried to crawl to her favorite tree. "Oh no! I can't crawl anymore. My legs are broken!" Cathy moaned. A quiet voice said to Cathy, "Your legs are not broken. There's no need to crawl anymore. Use your wings." Cathy asked,

"Who are you? Are you the same butterfly Messenger who was in my dream?" The Messenger answered, "Cathy, my name is Coach," she said warmly. "I am here to guide you on your new path. I've helped many butterflies evolve." As Cathy turned her head and looked back at her long body, she realized she had a beautiful set of wings. She had become the creature she dreamed about!

Cathy flew to the tree where her friends gathered. When Cathy landed on the tree leaf, they admired her beauty but didn't know it was her. "Hi, guys! I'm back," Cathy said. "Oh, sounds like Caterpillar Cathy," they howled. "It's me! My new name is Butterfly Cathy. You can become a butterfly, too. It wasn't just a dream," she answered. She knew she was created to be a leader to help other caterpillars evolve. She wished to get help to become the best butterfly leader she could be.

Chapter 2: Wings of Influence

What comes to mind when you hear the word *"leader"?* There are leaders who care about others, and unfortunately, there are also leaders who do not act responsibly. Good leaders respect, value, and guide others towards making positive decisions. In a school setting, student leaders might serve in various roles, such as mentor, buddy, tutor, teacher's assistant, office assistant, safety patrol, peer mediator, cafeteria monitor, or class president. True leaders only follow a crowd if it is headed in the right direction. Bad leaders try to influence others towards actions that are harmful to themselves or others. Be sure to lead in the right direction. If you choose to follow someone, make sure the person is moving in a positive direction.

> **LEADER**
> One who directs or guides; a coach; a person who is in charge or a group; a person with authority and influence

12 Traits of Good Leaders

Many students ask, "What does a good leader look and act like?" Responsible leaders have these qualities:

- Vision—Leaders can see the big picture. They imagine and expect future success. Vision allows you to use the power of imagination to see your goal as if it's already achieved. Can you see success for yourself? You are designed for success. You may be in a single-parent home where your mother struggles to pay bills, or you may be in a home with both parents where there are other problems. Just because there is struggle now, does not mean you have to struggle when you grow up. Many successful adults (like athletes, business owners, and teachers) came from families with struggles and adversity. Some were in foster care. **See success for yourself!** I see it!

- Fairness–Great leaders can be fair and respectful to others despite their backgrounds and differences. When you are fair, you don't discriminate against someone because of race, appearance, grades, money (or lack thereof), ability, or disability. The person you discriminate against might be someone you need later. **Be fair to everyone. You would like others to be fair to you, too.**

- Self-control–Leaders manage their own behavior and emotions. They never say, "I can't help or control it." I've met with many students about their behavior who said, *"I can't change it or help it."* If you believe you can't control your actions or results, you will always be in trouble, you will always be a victim, and you will never live your best life. Also, you will become a target for others, and they will push your buttons to see you lose control. You can always do something to help yourself. **Take responsibility for your behavior and avoid the blame game.**

- Coachability–Are you willing to learn from others? Good leaders realize they don't know it all. They allow others to teach them. Believe it or not, I have a Coach. Every athlete has a coach and trainer. Every student has a teacher. You learned because someone coached you.

Chapter 2: Wings of Influence

Your family and teachers taught you to write and speak your language. There is always someone who knows more than you. **Be coachable and always willing to learn.**

- Responsibility–Great leaders make responsible choices. We trust them to do the right thing, even when no one tells them. They think about safety for themselves as well as others. They follow rules, take the expected action, and encourage others to do the same. **Be responsible wherever you are.**

- Focus–Leaders can focus on their goals even when those around them aren't. Let's talk about focus for a second. You love your phone, but do you need it when reading and studying? We all like having fun and chatting with friends. The phone stops a lot of students from focusing and being successful. You are smarter than your phone. **When it's time to complete a task at home or school, focus instead of allowing your phone or games to control you.**

- Goals and planning–Leaders set goals and create a plan. **Set your goal and then plan how to accomplish it.**

- Action–Leaders take steps toward their goals. **After you create your plan – take action.**

- Able to handle constructive criticism–Constructive criticism is feedback that helps you improve. It helps you learn from mistakes and make positive changes. Good leaders listen for the truth in criticism because positive and negative feedback can help them grow. **Instead of being angry because someone criticizes you, be** thankful that someone cares enough to help you do better.

- Ability to make thoughtful choices—Good leaders think before they make choices. **Always consider the consequences before you say or do something.**

- Meaningful relationships—Good leaders hang around students who make good choices and care about character, respect, truth, academic success, and good citizenship. They avoid getting involved in petty stuff. Have you ever heard, "Birds of a feather flock together?" This means that girls who are alike hang together. If you hang around girls who curse and disrespect other students and teachers, you might do the same just to fit in. Hang around students you admire. **Surround yourself with people who make good choices so you won't have regrets.**

- Positive thinking—Great leaders think a certain way. According to research, you think over 50,000 thoughts a day, many of which are negative and harmful. It's not surprising that negative thinking often leads to unwanted outcomes. Imagine the possibilities if you became aware of your thought patterns and trained yourself to think more positively. If your thoughts were more positive, do you believe your experiences at school and home would improve? A famous proverb states, "As a man thinks in his heart, so is he." This suggests that your thoughts shape your life. Your thoughts influence your feelings, actions, and, your outcomes. Instead of believing thoughts like "I'm a loser," adopt a more positive mindset by thinking, "I've got this! I will be a star student." Set your expectations high and expect success! **Choose to think positive and helpful thoughts.**

Young Leaders Who Changed the World

You are not too young to make a difference. Many young people changed the world! Take a look at the videos about student leaders. What stands out about them? (QR codes are also provided for a video of each leader.)

Traci Weinstein:
- (1) https://bitly.ws/35ecQ
- (2) https://bitly.ws/35edt

Marie Keller
1. https://bitly.ws/35eeH
2. https://bitly.ws/35eg4

Makaila Umber
1. https://bitly.ws/35egw
2. https://bitly.ws/35ef7

Jennifer Bricker
1. https://bitly.ws/35ehr
2. https://bitly.ws/35ehH

Traci Weinstein	Marie Keller	Makaila Umber	Jennifer Bricker

You, as a Leader

You were drawn to this book because you are also a leader. What changes would you make if you could change the world, your community, or your school? There is a leader in you. You will do something great that will leave a mark and a memory for others. This is the reason you seem or feel different. Like the other kids you just saw, there's something special about you and in you! *You are going to use your wings to do big things!*

LEADERSHIP INVENTORY

1. You have learned twelve (12) important traits of leaders. List the traits you have.

_____

_____

_____

2. Can you think of other traits that are not mentioned that good (effective) leaders have?

_____

_____

_____

Chapter 2: Wings of Influence

3. Which traits are missing in your life? Or which leadership traits would you like to improve?

_____

_____

_____

4. What are some examples of "bad" leadership?

_____

_____

_____

5. How have you made a difference (or how are you making a difference) in your school, family, and community?

_____

_____

_____

_____

6. How will you make a difference in the future?

_____

_____

_____

_____

What Would You Do?

This morning, as you entered your class, you were greeted by a surprise: a substitute teacher was in charge. She seemed very nice and easygoing. However, your friends and classmates quickly took advantage of the situation and began to act out. They started disrespecting her, throwing books, saying nasty things, and running through the halls. The substitute teacher in tears. What action would you take in this situation?

Remember this…

Young leaders come in all shapes, sizes, and colors and they come from various backgrounds. If you want to see what a leader looks like, look in the mirror! You might lead at school, home, church, or on your sports team. Continue leading in the right direction and stay focused and coachable.

CHAPTER 3: BUTTERFLY BRAIN POWER – Secrets to School Success

As Cathy rested on the flower, Coach urged her to enroll in Butterfly Academy. Cathy was thrilled about attending school. She also felt that school would push her out of her comfort zone and help her learn even more. However, Cathy struggled to achieve good grades, while her friends made the honor roll. She knew she was smart but wondered if she was missing something important. Seeking advice, Cathy flew to Coach. With a low tone and eyes cast downward, she confessed, "Coach, I'm excited about school, but I'm not sure how to excel. I'm struggling and making C's and D's. What should I do?" Coach replied, "Cathy, to improve your grades, you need to find out why you are struggling. It might be necessary to change your study habits and seek additional help." Motivated by Coach's advice, Cathy decided it was time to focus and get to work.

The Day I Cried in Kenya

One day, while riding in the matatu (public transportation van) in Kenya, I looked out the window and saw a group of children walking to school. I noticed that the bottoms of their feet looked similar. It appeared they were wearing shoes with black soles. As we moved closer, I noticed they weren't wearing shoes! The bottoms of their feet were black from the stain of black tar on the roads they walked on day after day. As we moved even closer, the driver explained that these children walk miles daily to go to school with heavy books in their arms. They seemed content as they walked, talked, and smiled at one another. When I made eye contact with them, I waved, and they waved back with a smile.

As they smiled, tears filled my eyes and streamed down my cheeks. This was a memory I would never forget. So many thoughts raced through my mind at that moment. They committed themselves to learning even though they had to walk miles to school barefoot. My heart sank at the sight of their small, shoeless feet. I could only imagine how uncomfortable the hot tar felt against their tender soles. After their long journey, they arrived at a school that lacked electricity and running water.

During my month-long stay in Kenya, I met other young children like them. Even though they lived in conditions of poverty, they had a positive attitude and a wealth of discipline,

Chapter 3: Butterfly Brain Power

commitment, and focus. A teacher I met explained that by third grade, the children at her school spoke three languages (Swahili, French, and English) and had already begun learning algebra. I wish all students and parents had this level of dedication to education.

Our children here in America are so fortunate. As a student, you go to a school that has heat, air conditioning, food, floors, desks, bathrooms, water, a nurse, and electricity. Upon arrival, breakfast is available. Transportation is provided to and from school. Even though students can ride a school bus, some stay at home. You can access computers, technology, books, and the materials you need to learn. Some schools offer free school supplies, backpacks, and uniforms. Even with these provisions, many do not appreciate or value education. Many parents and students here in the U.S. do not know what students and parents in other countries sacrifice for education.

When I shared this story with my students during a guidance lesson, one replied, "So, there is no excuse for us to fail! We've got everything." Another student said, "Wow! I didn't know other kids go through so much to go to school!" The moral of this true story is, "You don't have to fail! If you don't have what you need, resources are available to you."

What's the Purpose of School?

Believe it or not, school prepares you for life and your future job. You practice social skills, learn to get along with classmates, build relationships with people who will become lifetime friends, and learn to follow routines and rules. There's a time to start your day, a time for bathroom breaks, a time to eat lunch, and a time to begin each subject. You certainly learn the importance of time management.

School is where many students learn to read and write for the first time. You may have started reading or learned to write your name before you started school, but many learn this at school.

Your strengths and weaknesses become clearer as you take new classes. You spend most of your day learning information that you will test on later. As you learn new subjects, it becomes clear to you what your strengths are. You may discover that math concepts are easy for you to understand. Or you may discover that you love reading, but dislike writing. You also learn more about yourself, your personality, communication style, and behavior.

School introduces you to activities, the arts, sports, and clubs. You have the opportunity to participate and discover what you are passionate about.

School helps you learn time management. Practicing time management includes being on time for school. Even with good grades, excessive absences can lead to repeating the grade or attending summer school. School attendance is so important that your parents can get in trouble, go to truancy court, and go to jail if you don't attend! I am aware of instances where parents served jail time because their children missed too many school days. Be sure to attend school regularly, engage in learning, and strive for academic excellence. If you have access to a school bus, you don't have to rely on a parent to take you to school. We realize you can't drive, but do what you can to help your parent leave the house on time if they are responsible for taking you to school. Occasionally, parents might also need help with their time management skills.

Why All the Fuss About Grades?

You hear your teachers, counselor, parents, principal, and assistant principal talk about grades all the time, right? There may be a lot of pressure or conversation about grades. You might even say, "Grades aren't everything." Other things are important too, but your grades will follow you, open doors for you, or close doors. Grades tell a story!

Grades show what you did during the last marking period. The day that report cards go home can be a good or bad day for students. Some students are happy because their hard work and focus paid off. They will receive a reward and lots of praise. But for some students, the report card could mean punishment and loss of privileges such as (cell phone, games, TV, and playing with friends).

Grades help determine if you have learned the information your teachers taught. After you learn new information, teachers test you to see if you understand. Grades also help your teacher see where she needs to review or re-teach.

While we are talking about grades, let's take a moment to address standardized and state tests. When I tested students, I noticed that some rushed because they wanted to finish first. The ones who rushed did not take the test seriously. They were the ones who had crazy low scores! Some had low scores because they clicked on answers without reading the questions. Here's what I want you to know: It is better to take your time, go through the test, and do your best so that you have to test once instead of having to do a re-take and risk failing.

Educators make decisions about you, your intelligence, and your abilities based on your grades. The classes or activities you take (or will be allowed to take) will depend on your grades.

Your grades allow you to participate in other activities or sports. Some clubs or school programs require certain grades. If you want to play sports, you have to make acceptable grades. Coaches feel that sports will be a distraction if you already have low grades.

Education is the key to finding a job. Passing grades are the key to getting a high school diploma! Some companies will not hire people who are high school dropouts. Did you know that students who drop out of school are more likely to experience unemployment (no job, no money), early pregnancy, crime, violence, drug abuse, emotional crisis, depression, and anxiety?

How to Be Successful in School

Our Evolved Girl Ambassador Ramani shares tips on how you can shine in school. But first, here's a little info about Ramani.

Chapter 3: Butterfly Brain Power

She is an 11th grader, has 7 siblings, and is the oldest girl. She is a hard worker at school, at home, and in her community. Ramani's mom is a single parent and works hard as well.

Ramani has become an Honor Roll student, deeply committed to her education and achieving high grades. To support herself, she works two jobs, helping to cover fees for extracurricular activities and other necessities. Despite her frequent smiles, Ramani has faced disappointments and struggles that are uncommon for the average student. When she transferred to a new middle school mid-year, her grades suffered, placing her at risk of failing. She was at a breaking point and felt like giving up. However, Ramani chose to attend summer school to get back on track. She promised herself that she would not let her grades drop that low again. She was determined to succeed!

Ramani has demonstrated academic excellence, respect, vision, community service, and a willingness to learn. She transformed her mindset, grades, and attitude. Now, Ramani inspires other young girls. Today, she is a cheerleader, member of the National Honor Roll Society, and Class President. Ramani says, "Here's how to be successful in school:"

- Create a strong bond with your teachers, counselors, and principals.
- Have a mind of your own, and don't follow others. Be a leader and be yourself.
- Stay out of the way of mess and don't get involved in a mess you don't belong in.
- Get involved in extracurricular activities.
- Surround yourself with people that you can be yourself with. Choose your friends wisely.
- Go to class on time. Don't play in the halls when you know there are consequences to being late!
- Be respectful.
- Choose to keep good grades. Desire to win. Here are some tips on making good grades:
  - Take notes in your own words so that you understand them.
  - Get involved with the lesson by asking questions. Don't be afraid to ask questions.

- Study! Don't wait until the night before a test to study; that's too late. Start studying the day that you find out about the test.

How to Transform Your Grades

Ramani provided great advice about school and grades. Here are some other tips that you can add to your tool kit:

- **Ask for help.** If you are not doing well, tell your parents and teachers you need help. We all need help at some point. Failing and not trying to get help is not a smart move! Talk to your teacher and ask if she can help you or allow someone in class can tutor you. Just because you are failing does not mean that you are not smart. You may need to learn a different way or do something differently. Be sure to ask for help before it's too late so that you won't drown!

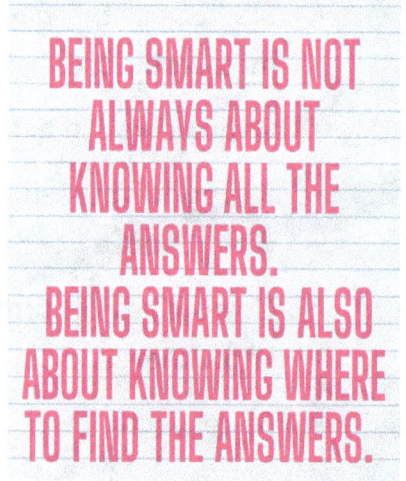

- **Do your homework!** Stop and take the time to do homework. Even if you don't have homework, study at home. Some students will only study if someone makes them do it. Be a big girl and learn those math formulas and vocabulary words. If you struggle with a subject, you can find a YouTube tutorial to explain it.

- **Make an appointment with your counselor.** Let him (or her) know you need help. Your counselor will help you create a plan and action steps.

- **Change your habits.** What are your habits when you get up in the morning or when you come home from school? When you get home from school, do you relax, get a snack, and begin homework? Or do you have fun and ignore homework? Be sure to create habits that help you, not habits that hurt you. Self-control and good habits are necessary if you want to make good grades.

- **Create a study routine.** Do you have a specific study time? Consider when, where, and how you study. Do you study better in a quiet space where concentration is possible? Or do you attempt to study in a distracting environment filled with noise from the TV, music, or crying siblings? It's important to select a location that enables you to focus and fully understand the material you are studying.

- **Test yourself.** After you read something, test yourself to see if you can remember and understand what you just read. If you cannot remember or explain what you read, you are not focusing or comprehending. It may be necessary to change your environment or the way that you study.

- **Turn off distractions and focus.** When you study, turn off your cell phone, tablet, and TV. You must be able to focus if you want to do well.

- **Go to bed on time.** I know you hate to hear this; you need 8 – 10 hours of sleep. If you don't get enough sleep, it affects your ability to think, understand, and process information. If you are not alert at school, it will be hard to understand easy stuff!

- **Find out who is doing well in your class and ask them what they are doing to get good grades.** Perhaps they can coach you. Don't feel embarrassed. Embarrassment will cause you to stay behind.

- **Rule out vision problems.** When your teacher is writing on the board or showing information on the Smartboard, can you see it? I have met with students who were having a hard time reading and understanding because they could not see well. When the nurse tested their vision, they realized they needed eyeglasses. If you are not doing well, know all the reasons!

Why Is Reading So Important?

Some students love to read. They get excited about getting new or used books. There are also students who hate to read. Can I tell you something? *Reading will always be required, no matter what you do or where you go.* When you apply for a job, you have to read the application. When you go to a restaurant, there's a menu to read. When it's time to drive, you must read the driver's manual and take a test. If you are going to college, you will read many books. If you are a student who does not like to read, I hope you will change your thoughts about reading and see it as something necessary for your growth. Get into the habit of reading. The more you read, the more you will learn. As you read more, you will feel comfortable.

My colleague, Mrs. Cassandra East, is a Reading Intervention Coach in Mobile County Public Schools. She said this:

> "The love of reading can be an open path to a successful school year and beyond. A vibrant and avid reader can understand the text and see through the author's eyes. Avid means having an interest and enthusiasm. Reading is a part of every subject that you will take in school. If you can understand what you read, there's a better chance of you passing that class. Strive to become a fluent reader. Fluent reading means you can read the text at a good pace and understand what you are reading. If you are a fluent reader, you have a better chance of becoming a fluent writer, which allows you to express yourself. So, please take the time to read and watch the world open."

A Reading Tip from Sofie

When 10th grader Sofie has trouble following a book, she listens to it on audiobook or on YouTube while reading along. This also helps her learn how to pronounce unfamiliar words. Sofie says to read whatever you're interested in, including graphic novels. If you're not sure what you might like, ask your friends for ideas. Join or start a book club with them. She finds recommendations on "BookTok" (TikTok).

Chapter 3: Butterfly Brain Power

Managing Math

Math is one of the subjects that many students struggle with. Some wish they could avoid math forever! There are fun and interesting things about math! Counting money, managing your bank account or debit card, and shopping online are examples of math activities.

Ms. Latangula Bell, a Math Invention Coach in Mobile County Public Schools, says this:

"Often, there's a negative stereotype about girls' capabilities in mathematics. Let me encourage you to:

- Be confident. Confidence will play a huge role in you becoming and remaining successful in mathematics.

- Think positive. Transform any negative thoughts or notions that you or others may have about your intelligence when it comes to mathematics. Mindset plays a big part in your relationship with math. If you begin your class or math assignment with negative feelings, you'll be stuck and defeated before you begin.

- Find other resources. Khan Academy.org is a good resource for math. It offers free online assistance with math starting with Pre-K through college. YouTube is another resource where you can find tutorials.

- Don't give up. You can evolve into whoever you want to be in life. You are in control of your future.

What's Your Smart?

Students are smart in different ways. Unfortunately, schools only measure intelligence (and abilities) in subjects like reading, language, science, and math. You might do very well in science or math but need help in language arts or English. Don't let that discourage you. You will only be a genius in some things. Everyone has an area where they shine. You do, too!

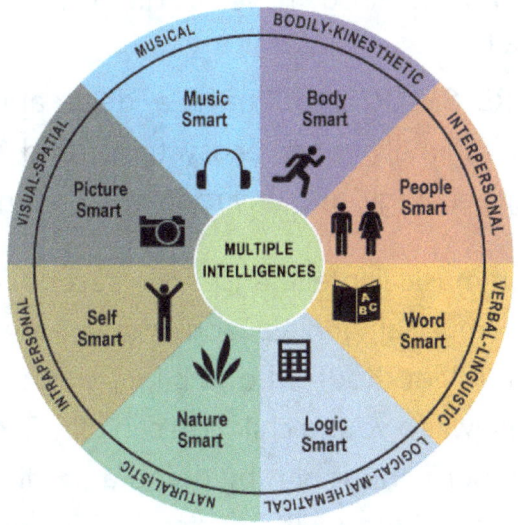

According to Psychologist Howard Gardner, there are several types of intelligence or ways in which you are smart:

- WORD SMART: You do well in writing, speaking, storytelling, and languages.
- LOGIC SMART: You do well in math and problem-solving.
- PICTURE SMART: You do well in understanding visual data. Artists and architects are picture-smart.

- **MUSIC SMART:** You are great at playing instruments, composing music, singing, and recognizing patterns you hear.
- **BODY SMART:** Athletes, dancers, surgeons, and actors are body smart.
- **PEOPLE SMART:** You are good at reading emotions, empathizing, and building relationships.
- **SELF SMART:** You have a deep understanding of yourself.
- **NATURE SMART:** You have a deep appreciation for plants, animals, and ecosystems and subjects like biology, ecology, and environmental science.

Let's talk about musical intelligence for a second. Kodi Lee is an example of a musical genius. You may have seen him on America's Got Talent. Kodi, who is blind, was diagnosed with Autism when he was a young child. He can play five instruments. You can learn more about him by doing a (Kodi Lee) search at www.youtube.com. Others with musical intelligence are Michael Jackson, Prince (who played 27 instruments on an album), Mozart, Beethoven, Stevie Wonder, and Paul McCartney.

What are your main areas of intelligence? Do your friends come to you when they need advice? You are people smart if you are good at solving people's problems and giving advice. Or you may be a natural-born athlete (body smart.) Perhaps, you understand math problems with ease. It is great to understand your brilliance because this is the area you will build on. Your extracurricular activities will connect with your strengths.

Understanding "how" you are smart will remove the pressure of believing that you have to be perfect in everything.

ACADEMICS INVENTORY

1. What are your thoughts about learning?
   _____
   _____
   _____

2. Do you enjoy school? _____

3. What are your grades in each of your classes?
   _____
   _____
   _____

4. Do you feel good about your grades? _____

5. If your grades are low, are you doing everything that you can to be successful such as doing homework, reading, getting tutored, watching videos about the subject, and putting the phone down so that you can focus?

6. Do you complete your homework when it is assigned? _____

7. When your grades are low, do you ask your teachers, friends, or parents for help? _____

Chapter 3: Butterfly Brain Power

8. Do you have a daily routine for studying? _____

9. Do you enjoy reading? _____ Do you enjoy math? _____

10. When you learned about the areas of intelligence, which one(s) did you connect with the most?
_____

_____

_____

Remember this...

You are in control of your success, and failure does not have to be an option. You have the potential to excel in school and achieve grades that make you proud. Identify what's preventing you from performing at your best. Once you've figured out what's standing in your way, develop a strategy to win the grade game!

If you're a student who is making good grades, consider becoming a tutor in your classroom to assist others. If you're interested in helping your peers, talk to your teacher (and parents) about supporting a classmate who is facing challenges. This is what Evolved Girls do!

CHAPTER 4: DREAM BIG AND FLY HIGH —The Guide to Achieving Your Goals

Coach explained to Cathy that success doesn't happen on its own; it requires a plan. "Butterfly Cathy, I'll teach you how to set goals so you can achieve your dream. Research proves that individuals who set goals and write them are more likely to succeed. Dreaming without action is just wishing," Coach said. Butterfly Cathy picked up her twig pencil and started to jot down her goals. As she listed her goals, she realized she was unsure about how to achieve them. Knowing the steps to take would help turn some of her dreams into reality. She confessed to Coach, "I've written down my goals, but I'm not sure what comes next." Coach put her and ease and said, "Cathy, I'll show you the way!" Cathy responded with enthusiasm, "Learning this now, Coach, could change my life forever!"

Chapter 4: Dream Big and Fly High

Why Students Don't Accomplish Their Goals

Have you ever wondered why some students accomplish goals and others don't? There is an art to accomplishing your goals. Wishing and daydreaming will not help you achieve a goal. Here are reasons that students don't accomplish goals:

- *Lack of goals.* Some students live from day to day with no goal in mind.

- *Lack of action and planning.* If you have a goal but no plan, you won't achieve the goal. After you create your plan, you must take action. Winning involves doing something! You can't win a game if you don't participate.

- *Lack of confidence and faith in themselves.* Confidence is knowing you are able; faith is knowing that you can and will despite your current reality.

- *Lack of support.* I have met students who told me that no one believed in them or they didn't get help from home. Don't get discouraged by the negative beliefs that people have about you. If an adult does not believe in you, don't let that stop you from dreaming. There is someone who believes in you! It may be a teacher, a friend, or a family member. Believe the ones who believe in you!

- *Hiding out.* Some students try to hide their intelligence and talent. They feel they must "dumb down" to be accepted by their peers. If you hang with friends who don't appreciate your intelligence and uniqueness, it might be time to choose new friends. Don't shrink to make someone else feel good. Be who you are, humbly. Be powerful!

How SMART is Your Goal?

Many schools teach students about SMART goals. In November 1981, George T. Doran introduced SMART goals. A goal is SMART if it is:

- Specific: A goal is specific if it is clear and you know exactly what you want to accomplish. Your goals should answer, *"what, why, when, and where."*

- Measurable: A goal is measurable if you can track it to know when it is accomplished. This will involve numbers or data. *Examples of a measurable goal are: I will raise my grade from a C to a B. I will earn $50 from chores by the end of the month.*

- Achievable: Your goal is achievable if you know it is possible to complete, even if it seems difficult.

- Relevant: A goal is relevant if it is important to you and worth your while.

- Timely: Your goal needs a set time (date) that you expect to accomplish it.

How to Make Your Dreams Come True

You have been setting goals since you were a small kid. Have you ever asked your parents for a toy or something special? Were you showing good behavior or being extra nice so you could convince your parents to take you to McDonalds? Maybe you did more chores with the hopes of influencing your parents to give into your wish! This was an example of you working hard to make your dream come true. Here's the process to accomplish your goal now: **identify your goal, see your goal, create a plan, and take action.**

IDENTIFY YOUR GOAL

You learned from the SMART goal model that you must be clear about your goal. You are never too young to dream big and set goals. Your job is to identify your important goals. When I ask students about goals, many feel they should choose something they want to buy (like clothes, games, or pets). Your goal might be different, like making the honor roll, meeting new friends, starting a kid business, or finding a forever home. Your goals will most likely be in one of more of the following areas: *grades, behavior, friends, family, health, and fun.* Choose the goals that are important to you and write them below.

1. Academics / Grades

_____

_____

_____

2. Behavior

_____

_____

_____

3. Friendships / Relationships

_____

_____

_____

4. Family / Home
_____
_____
_____

5. Health
_____
_____
_____

6. Extracurricular activities (fun, recreation)
_____
_____
_____

SEE YOUR GOAL

Bill Gates, the co-founder of Microsoft Corporation, has significantly influenced global technology. From middle school, Mr. Gates had a vision and an interest in shaping technology, engaging actively in computing, and coding. This book was written using Word, a product of Microsoft. Other notable Microsoft products and services include Teams, Outlook, and Internet Explorer.

Success often comes to those who set goals, plan, and visualize their achievements. Visualization is a powerful technique for creating a mental image of a desired outcome. It helps you to maintain focus and see a goal as if it has already been achieved. This method is not only popular among successful athletes but also widely practiced by business professionals.

In a study, Russian scientists compared four groups of Olympic athletes. They were compared by two types of training programs: physical training and mental training. The physical training program included physical exercises and workouts. The mental training included visualizing (seeing a picture of success in your mind).

- Group 1 received 100% physical training, which means working out.

- Group 2 received 75% physical training and 25% mental training.

- Group 3 received 50% physical training with 50% mental training.

- Group 4 received 25% physical training with 75% mental training.

Which group do you believe had the best performance? Group 4, who did 25% physical training and 75% visualizing, performed the best. The athletes discovered that visualization (imagined success) affected their muscular impulses.

Set aside at least five minutes every day to visualize (see) your goal. Close your eyes and see yourself there, as if it is happening now. *What are you doing? How do you feel?* You'll bring into your existence the resources needed to accomplish your goal.

CREATE A PLAN

A goal without a plan is like a bicycle without wheels! It won't move. A plan is the action or steps you will take to achieve your goal. Every goal needs a plan! Be sure to write out your plan and include the steps you will take. If you want to make new friends, change your behavior, get along with others, or get better grades, you must create a plan. See the example below.

<u>Example of a S.M.A.R.T goal and plan for behavior</u>

I will manage my temper and change my behavior in 14 days. I will not disrupt class or talk loudly when I am angry. This goal is SPECIFIC, MEASURABLE, ACHIEVABLE, RELEVANT, and TIMELY.

TAKE ACTION

What happens after you have a goal and a plan? The next step is to *take action!* You can have a big dream, a great goal, and a perfect plan, but if you don't take the next step, nothing will happen. Winners are not afraid to take the next step. What is the next step for you? Who are the people that can help you take action? Remember to ask for help when you need it. Here are the action steps for the goal above:

Action Plan 1: Use a calm and quiet voice to say "stop" to a student who is bothering me.

Action Plan 2: If this does not work, I will ignore the student instead of giving her my attention.

Action Plan 3: If the problem continues, I will tell the teacher and ask for advice.

Action Plan 4: I can ask the school counselor for a meeting with the other student so that we can discuss this.

*When students meet face-to-face, they can talk freely and address their differences and misunderstandings that created the conflict. Often, students left my office as friends when we met to discuss a conflict they were having.

Action Plan 5: If this does not work, I will ask my parents to plan a conference with the teacher and the principal or assistant principal. If I feel that it's necessary, I will go to the office to request a meeting with my principal or assistant principal.

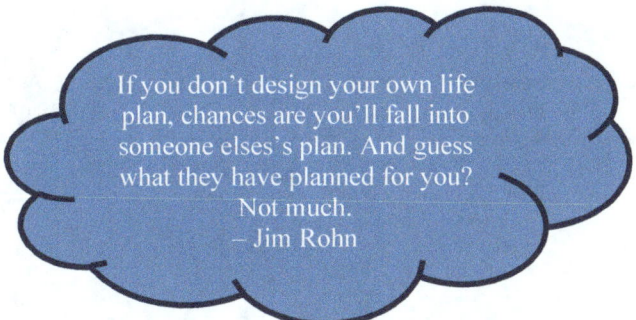

If you don't design your own life plan, chances are you'll fall into someone elses's plan. And guess what they have planned for you?
Not much.
– Jim Rohn

In the previous example, the student started small with a 2-week goal. You might ask, *"What if I don't know where or how to start?"* You could ask your parents, school counselor, or teacher for help.

Chapter 4: Dream Big and Fly High

Goal-Mapping

There are different tools or methods you can use to create your plan. One way to create a plan is to use a goal map. A goal map is a tool that breaks your goal into small action steps or tasks. We could also use a goal map for the previous behavior goal. You would put the goal in the middle and then identify steps to achieve the goal. Here's an example of goal map along with steps to take.

Example: If you want to improve your math grade, you can create a goal map like the one below.

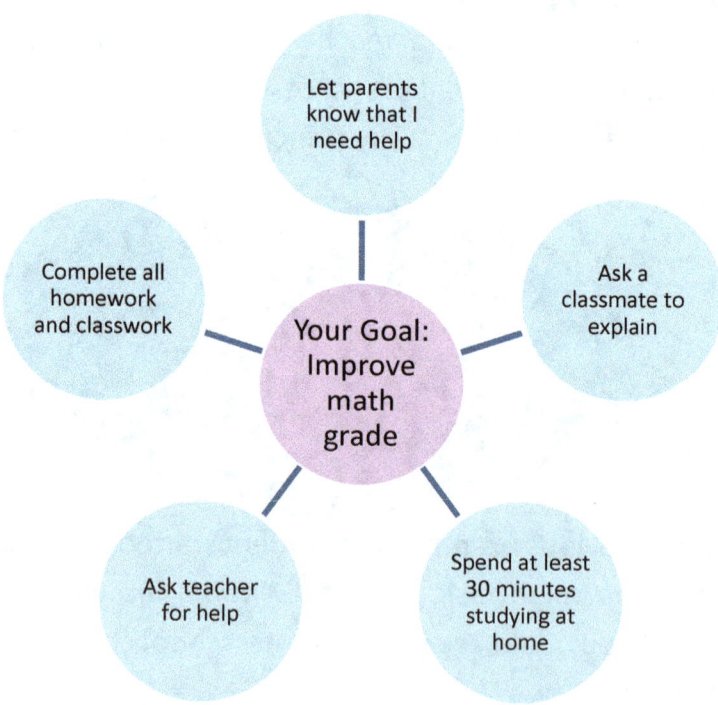

GOAL MAP WORKSHEET

You identified a goal earlier. Use the goal map below to write your goal and identify the steps to accomplish it.

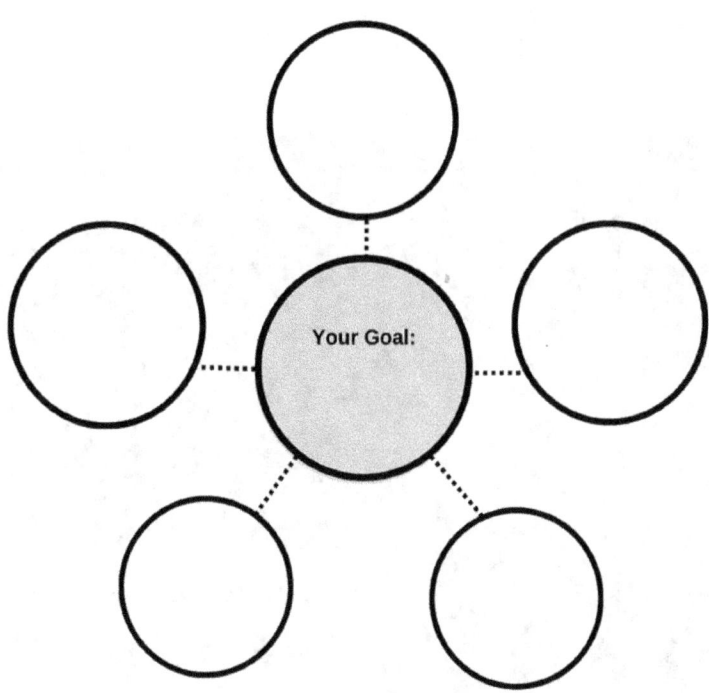

How to Bake Dreams into Reality

There's no such thing as being too young to pursue your dreams or start something incredible! Don't let fear take control; instead, use your talents and creativity to shine. If you have a big goal, now is the perfect time to take that exciting first step towards making it happen.

Chapter 4: Dream Big and Fly High

Meet Mani! She is an honor roll student and an example of an evolved girl who knows how to set a goal, plan, and act upon it. Passionate about baking delicious desserts and sweet treats since the third grade, she started her sweet journey baking cupcakes and red velvet cakes. Encouraged by a friend to take her baking skills seriously, Mani, now in the 8th grade, earns money for her sweetness!

After she realized that she could earn dough by following her passion, she decided to take her baking to the next level. She came up with a cool business name and whipped up a mouthwatering dessert menu for her business.

When I talked to Mani, she gave some awesome advice for others who want to be a "Girl Boss" and bake their dreams into reality. Here's what she said with her sweet self:

- Don't be scared! Don't give up on your business. The beginning is hardest. Put your best effort into it.
- Make it easy for people to support your business. I had a straightforward list where people knew upfront the products and costs. People shouldn't have to go through a maze to find your products.
- If you have a passion for something, you should follow it. Yes, follow your heart and mind. If you're not passionate about something, don't do it.
- Be respectful.
- Be organized. You can't have a business without organization. I had to have a system in place so that people could communicate with me about my products.
- Don't allow people to tell you what you can't do!

My Future Goals

I would like to learn how other bakers master their work. I believe I should learn skills from a business school and a pastry school. A business person needs two sets of skills: business skills so that you can run the business and specific training for the products you are selling.

Chapter 4: Dream Big and Fly High

The Power of a Planner

Mani understands the importance of planning. Have you ever used a planner? A planner is a tool to help organize your life and daily activities. It also allows you to track the tasks that relate to your goal.

Amy was a C and D student who needed to be more motivated. She had low grades because she missed assignments. She was okay with being "average." After she joined the Evolved Girl group, she realized she was settling for low grades and she wanted to do better. She changed her mind set about success. She made the A/B Honor Roll for the first time at the end of the marking period! She felt so good about her accomplishment. When she came to see me, she lit up as she talked about her success. I asked her how she improved her grades. She explained that she bought a planner to organize herself. After using a planner, she felt less stressed because she was not caught off guard with tests and assignments. She planned her study time, fun time, and work time. You can benefit from a planner too! Remember, we created the Evolved Girl Planner especially for you. Get your planner (at www.evolvedyou.net) to help you stay on track.

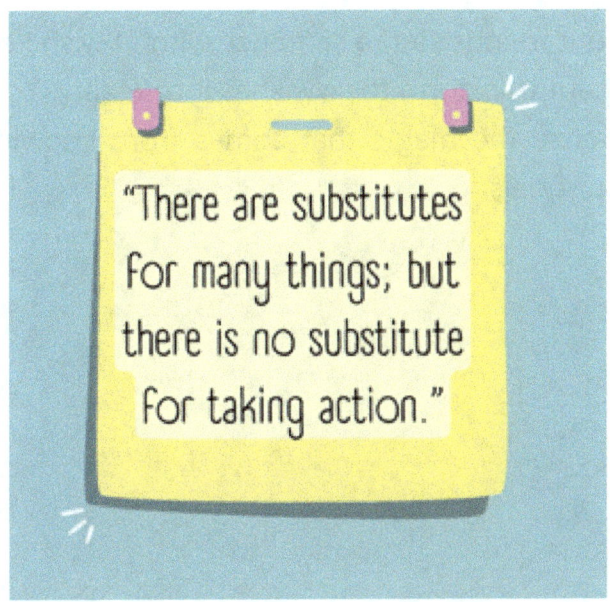

What Would You Do?

You didn't turn in two assignments because you forgot. You have been relying on your memory. What can you do to keep track of assignment due dates, test dates, special activities, and birthday party events? What would an Evolved Girl do?

Remember this...

You have learned the secret to accomplishing your goals! This powerful knowledge will benefit you for the rest of your life! This is information that some adults pay thousands of dollars to learn! You can now coach others on how to get results. When

Chapter 4: Dream Big and Fly High

you hear your friends start a sentence with, "I wish I could," you can help them transform their wishes into reality. You can soar and experience the magic that comes from knowing *how* to achieve your goals.

CHAPTER 5: WORTHY WINGS – Embracing Your Value

While Coach and Cathy flew to the garden, Coach felt that it was a good time to discuss the importance of value. She gently said, "Cathy one of the greatest gifts you can give yourself is knowing and appreciating your value. Many butterflies still see themselves as caterpillars. They forget they can use their beautiful wings to fly. They also forget they are smart enough to migrate in the direction they need for survival. So, you must know your value, Cathy. You are smart, talented, beautiful, and unique. There is no other butterfly in the world like you! When you love yourself, it will guide your actions. You will respect yourself and others. You will also appreciate who you are. You won't have to wait for others to tell you how special, smart, and outstanding you are because you will already know."

Chapter 5: Worthy Wings

Know Your Worth

Have you ever visited a museum? If so, you might have noticed how the items on display are protected to prevent them from being touched or damaged. Usually, there's information available explaining the importance of each item. The Smithsonian in Washington, D.C., is recognized as the world's largest museum complex. It houses a collection of precious documents, artifacts, exhibits, and art from around the world.

Believe it or not, you share something in common with these museums: something within you is incredibly valuable and deserves protection. You are as precious as a rare diamond! You have a unique and beautiful soul, with talent, creativity, intelligence, and personality. Just as each fingerprint is unique, so are you. In countless ways, you are valuable!

Throughout my years as a school counselor, I've met students who remembered hearing discouraging words from their parents, such as, "You're going to end up like your momma! You're not going to amount to anything in life!" Even if a parent or family member doubts your success, you have the ability to prove them wrong. Their words do not determine your future or your worth, you do! You are the architect of your own destiny!

Beauty is YOU!

I notice a big problem with many school girls; they don't know their value! Many girls allow others to define their worth, value, and beauty. They even allow others to set the standard for beauty. We have allowed the media to tell us what and who beauty is. The problem with this is you compare yourself to others. Don't buy the lie! Love the color of your skin. Beauty is YOU! Beauty is your skin, eyes, nose, and mouth. There is beauty in every race, every hair texture, and every shade. Appreciate not only your inner beauty, but your outward beauty as well. Be proud of your hair, whether wavy, curly, kinky, straight, short, long, or thick. There is no such thing as bad hair. Who told you that?

If you know and believe you are beautiful, you will act beautiful. If you think you are ugly and worthless, your actions will reflect that. When you don't know your value, you limit yourself and make choices that are not in your best interest. When you know your worth, you will protect your name and your reputation. You won't allow others to mistreat or minimize you.

Ashley was a middle school student who made the decision that she was not going to allow anyone to minimize and determine her worth.

Ashley's Story

When I was in middle school, I had a crush on Patrick. He was tall and handsome. I hoped he had a crush on me, too. I soon had hurt feelings. He said that I was too skinny for him. I went to the grocery store and asked my dad to buy chocolate milk and fatty foods to help me gain weight. But then something happened. One of my friends asked, "Why are you going through all that to make him like you? You are better than that!" I realized I was not valuing myself. I was trying to undo myself, hoping to make him like me.

If you have a crush on someone or someone has a crush on you, and the person says you need to be smaller or bigger, have longer or shorter hair, leave that person alone! Give no one that much power in your life. If someone does not appreciate you for who you are, move on, baby! Don't let others decide your worth.

- *Self-concept* - the belief and image you have of yourself
- *Self-esteem* - the way that you value and see yourself

Build Your Self-Esteem

Building your self-esteem is an essential part of your personal growth. Ashley realized that she needed to build her self-esteem. She started to appreciate her own value after a friend highlighted her worth.

Girls from all ages struggle with self-esteem and issues that relate to their self-esteem. My awesome sister, Greta Hunt, is a school counselor at a middle school in the Atlanta metropolitan area. When I asked her about common issues that she is seeing with girls today, here's what she said:

The social media culture has placed unrealistic beauty expectations on young girls resulting in low self-esteem. Also, society has become focused on the outward appearance rather than the psychological and educational development of adolescents.

In addition to the pressure that comes from the social media culture and image, academic expectations can affect girls' self-esteem and feelings of worth. Often, more emphasis is placed on advanced and honors classes causing academic stress for many students. If this isn't enough, many of today's youth are having difficulty maintaining friendships due to lack of conflict management skills. When they have difficulty with friendships, this also affects the way they view themselves and their worth.

We can agree that girls struggle with low self-esteem for different reasons. Even though there may be many things you are dealing with now, you *can* develop and improve your self-esteem. Your self-esteem belongs to you! You don't have to wait for others to build you up or see your worth. Even though you want others to see you as cool, *fire,* and amazing, you must see and know for yourself that you are AMAZING!

Developing your self-esteem is an ongoing process. The value that you place on yourself is determined by your self-concept and your self-esteem. Your self-concept is the belief or image that you have of yourself. Your self-esteem refers to the way you see yourself. Here are some tips to build your self-esteem and embrace your value:

- **Become self-aware:** Understand your strengths, weaknesses, interests, and values. Self-awareness helps you know what makes you unique.

- **Have positive self-talk and thoughts:** Replace your negative self-talk with positive affirmations. Replace negative beliefs about yourself with positive ones. Only you can do this. No one can do this for you.

- **Set goals:** Setting and accomplishing goals improves self-esteem and confidence. (We talked about goals already.)

- **Embrace individuality**: It's okay to be different. Your uniqueness is what makes you valuable.

- **Surround yourself with positivity:** Seek positive and supportive relationships. They play a role in helping you feel more valuable.

- **Self-care:** Take pride in how you show up. Take care of your physical and mental health. We'll talk more about this later.

- **Go after your interests and passions**: Explore the things you love to do, whether they are academic, creative, or athletic. Participating in activities that you enjoy can boost your self-esteem.

- **Celebrate achievements**: Always celebrate your accomplishments, no matter how small. Sometimes, you must pat yourself on the back if no one else does.

- **Be resilient:** When you are resilient, you bounce back from challenges and tough situations. Challenges, setbacks, and failures are a part of life. Learn from these experiences and grow stronger. Please don't allow them to break you down.

- **Be a role model:** Show others what leadership, self-confidence, and self-respect look like. Other students in your school are watching your actions and attitude. Inspire them!

- **Express yourself:** Express yourself through art, music, writing, or any form of self-expression you enjoy. Self-expression can help you develop a strong sense of identity and self-worth, while also helping to reduce stress.

Chapter 5: Worthy Wings

The Benefits of Knowing Your Value!

A strong sense of self-worth is a foundation for personal growth and resilience. When you know your worth, you can navigate life's challenges. You'll build and keep meaningful relationships, accomplish goals, and contribute to society. So, what are the benefits of knowing your value?

- You believe in yourself.

- You know that you are on this earth for a reason.

- You respect and love yourself. It's your responsibility to love yourself.

- You respect and value others.

- You have less stress and anxiety.

- You don't allow others to control you.

- You avoid comparing yourself to others.

- You say "no" when you need to.

- You are equipped to make better decisions.

- You feel courageous and powerful enough to protect yourself if someone harms you.

- You ask for help when you need it.

MEASURE YOUR VALUE – WORKSHEET

You have just learned the benefits of valuing yourself. Now, it is time to pause and tell yourself the truth about how *you* value yourself. As you answer the questions below, be honest with yourself.

1. What do you believe about yourself?

2. Write 5 traits you like about yourself.

_____

_____

_____

_____

3. List 2 things that you love about your physical appearance.

_____

_____

_____

4. What makes you unique?

_____

_____

_____

Chapter 5: Worthy Wings

5. How do others view you?

_____

_____

_____

> **What Would You Do?**
>
> You don't feel very good about yourself. You wish you had more support from home. No one tells you that you are beautiful and smart. You feel as if others overlook you. What can you do to feel better about yourself?

Remember this...

Evolved Girl, you are so valuable! Consider this - butterflies play a big role in pollinating gardens by helping the production of new seeds for fruits and vegetables. Though butterflies are small wonders, they constantly help plants grow. They recognize their beauty, value, and purpose. Always remember, you are a beautiful wonder, just like the butterfly! You are destined to pollinate and grow your own life. Just as the butterfly contributes to the flourishing of gardens, you, too, will help others grow. The world needs you!

CHAPTER 6: BUTTERFLY CHARM – Winning with Habits, Attitude, and Manners

Cathy listened as Coach spoke. "You have done a great job on this journey. There are some thoughts I want to leave with you. The big butterflies that you admire are just like you. In fact, you are just as talented and intelligent as they are. You think that life is easier for them. Their mindset and habits have made life somewhat easier for them. Mindset is how you think. How you think affects your behavior. You can improve your experiences at school and home by changing your thoughts and creating good habits.

Your personal habits position you for success. There are good habits and bad habits. The habits that you become a servant to will either make life easier or harder. If you want to stay in the game, form habits that will help you win. Set your alarm, wake up early, eat breakfast, do your homework, set goals, plan, get ample sleep, and eat healthy. If you use good habits in your daily life, you will be successful," Coach said confidently. "That's good advice, Coach," Cathy remarked. "Make sure that you

Chapter 6: Butterfly Charm

have an excellent habitude, Cathy. Habitude refers to a combination of your habits and attitude. A good habitude will set you apart from others" Coach stated and then quietly flew away.

Everyone in the world has habits. A habit is a behavior you repeat. You do many things because of habit, i.e., bathe, brush your teeth, comb your hair, communicate on social media, and study when you get home from school.

Habits That Change Your Life

You are successful because of your daily habits. Identify and replace habits that work against you. Here are some habits that will help you live your best life:

- Managing your time
- Following routine
- Asking for help
- Speaking positively
- Organizing
- Listening
- Being disciplined

Managing Time

Good leaders manage their time and put first things first. When you have good time management skills, you show up to class on time, go to bed on time without

being told, and get out of bed when you wake up. When you are late, it makes others late, too. Pay attention to time.

Setting Routines

Routines are important because they provide structure. You have routines from the moment you wake up to the time you go to sleep. There are routines for getting ready for school, eating breakfast, walking to your bus, studying, and having fun.

Asking

Many students suffer in silence because they are afraid to ask for help. When you need help, ask someone who can provide it. If you're struggling to understand a lesson, be sure to ask your teacher for help. Many students have said that they don't ask questions or ask for help because they don't want to appear dumb or stupid. You might get a failing grade if you don't ask questions or figure things out. Would you rather your classmates hear you ask a question, or would you rather them know that received a failing grade? So, ask the question. Asking questions is a wise strategy. Pretending to understand when you don't is not. So be smart and ask for what you need.

Speaking Positively

Your words are powerful; they are like seeds that you plant. Your words will cause things to grow in your life. What do you say about yourself? Avoid making statements like, "I can't pass my class. I'm not smart. No one likes me. I'm ugly. I'm bad." Instead, say positive things about yourself. It is NOT okay to call yourself or others a name. Instead of calling someone a name, state what the person does. For instance, don't call someone dumb just because she is failing Social Studies. An Evolved Girl would say, "She is struggling in Social Studies."

> *My habits will make me better or break me. I choose to allow them to make me better. I will choose helpful and healthy habits.*

Organizing Yourself

Organization skills help you manage your responsibilities at school and home. You can organize yourself by using your planner and determining the most important tasks. Organize your study or class materials so that you can easily find them. If you constantly lose stuff, you need to become more organized. You can do this!

Listening

Listening is important because it helps you understand instructions, take good notes, and communicate. Have you experienced someone not paying attention to you while talking? How did this make you feel? Even though listening happens with the ears, it also happens with your body language and eyes. Get into the habit of listening and paying attention. This skill will help you in more ways than you can imagine.

Chapter 6: Butterfly Charm

Being Disciplined

Discipline refers to behaviors, attitudes, and habits that promote responsibility and growth. You are disciplined if you have self-control and good habits, and follow the rules at school and home.

Take Inventory of Your Habits

A businessman said, "Tell me your habits and I will tell you if you will be successful." Now is a good time to think about your habits. Successful students consistently use certain habits to help them achieve academic and personal goals. Complete the Habit Inventory. An inventory is a document that includes a list of items (questions) to help you see where you stand. As you answer the questions, be honest!

1. What are some good habits that you have?
_____
_____
_____
_____

2. Which habits are holding you back from success?
_____
_____
_____

Habit Inventory

What time do you go to sleep? _____

What time do you wake up in the morning? _____

Section A **(You can answer with minutes or hours.)**

1. How much time do you spend watching TV daily? ____

2. How much time do you spend on the Internet every day for recreation, like TikTok, social media, games, chatting, emailing, videos)? ____

3. How much time do you spend daily–talking on the phone or texting on the group chat? ____

4. How much time do you spend on gaming? ____

Total time you spend on Section A activities: ____

Section B

1. How much time do you spend exercising every day? ____

2. How much time do you spend reading daily? ____

3. How much time do you spend on homework? ____

4. How much time do you spend practicing your skill or talents? ____

Total time you spend on Section B activities: ____

If the total in Section B is larger than Section A, you are committed, disciplined and focused. You know the importance of good habits. If the total Section A is larger than Group B, it is a great idea to create new habits and increase the activities in Section B.

Chapter 6: Butterfly Charm

Manners

Manners refer to how you act with people. Manners will open doors or close doors. Students with good manners will have opportunities (to join clubs and activities) that other students won't have. See the chart below for examples of manners.

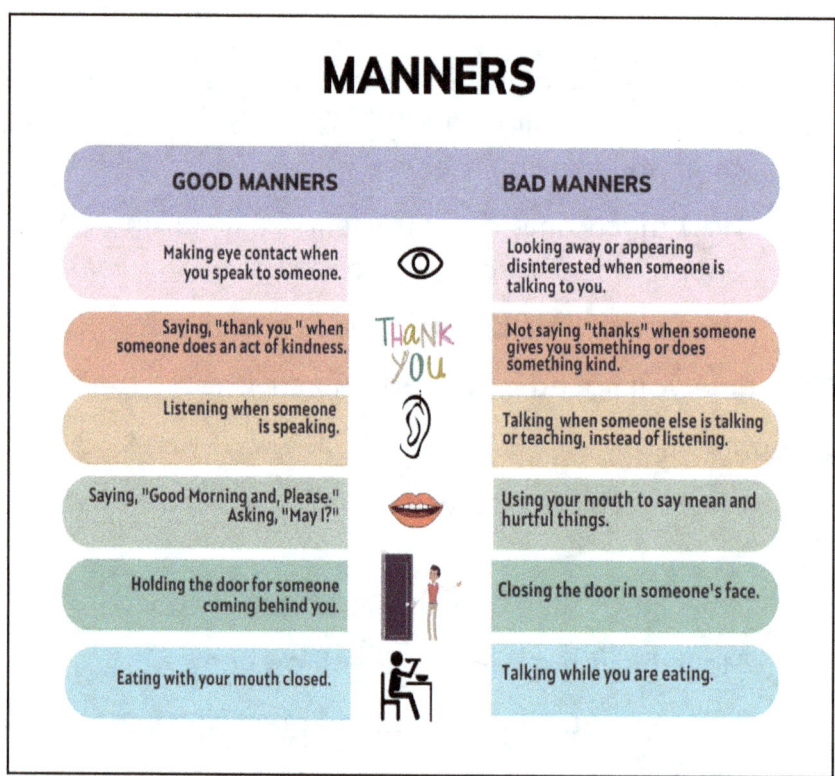

MANNERS WORKSHEET

1. What are some good manners that are not listed?
_____
_____
_____

2. What are some bad manners that are not listed?
_____
_____
_____

3. List good manners that you have.
_____
_____
_____

4. Do you say, "Please" or "May I" when you ask a question? (For example, if you want your classmate to share her potato chips, it is best to ask, "May I have some chips?" instead of saying, "Give me some chips.")
_____

5. Do you say, "thank you" when someone does some does a kind deed for you?
_____

6. List the manners you need to change:
_____
_____
_____

Chapter 6: Butterfly Charm

Have a Winning Attitude

Your attitude is a way of thinking or feeling that affects your behavior; it is how you show up at home, school, and in the world. What kind of attitude do you have when you wake up? Attitudes can be sour, pleasant, positive, or negative. You are the only person who gets to choose your attitude. There's nothing wrong with having an attitude, as long as it's a pleasant and winning attitude! Here are examples of how an attitude can open doors for you:

One day, the counseling office received a letter from a local university. They requested that we select two students who met the academic requirement of a 3.5-grade point average or higher to receive a full scholarship. When the other counselor and I met, we reviewed the list of eligible students. Several students had 4.00 averages! Surprisingly, we did not choose the students with a 4.0 average. Instead, we both agreed on Marissa. Every morning, Marissa greeted us with a "Good morning" and a warm smile. She always took the time to ask how I was doing. I will never forget her. She stood out because of her positive attitude and manners. While her grades made her eligible, it was her good attitude that unlocked the opportunity for a free education!

Examples of an Awesome Attitude	Examples of an Attitude Needing Improvement
- Believing that the glass is half full instead of half empty - Smiling and being kind to others - Showing gratitude for your blessings - Being a good sport even if your team is losing	- Thinking that no one likes you - Coming to class in a bad mood (not speaking to anyone) - Acting angry all the time - Quitting, fighting, or starting trouble if you lose a game

ATTITUDE INVENTORY

1. Who do you know that has a good attitude?

_____

_____

_____

2. What do you admire about their attitude?

_____

_____

_____

3. Do you know anyone with a sour attitude? How do others respond to this student?

_____

_____

_____

4. What kind of attitude do you have?

_____

_____

_____

5. Has anyone ever told you that you have a negative or bad attitude? _____

6. Is there anything that you need to do to improve your attitude?

_____

_____

What Would You Do?

You recently noticed you have a bad habit of talking about your classmates during lunchtime. You say a lot of negative things. The things that come out of your mouth are not very positive. How can you change the way that you communicate so that you are not a gossip or instigator?

Remember this...

The first thing that people notice about you is your attitude or your manners. Your attitude and manners reveal so much about you when you get on the bus, or walk into school, church, or a restaurant. People see your smile, your frown, and your body language before they have an opportunity to learn about you.

Chapter 7: Butterfly Harmony

CHAPTER 7: BUTTERFLY HARMONY – Handling Friendships, Girl Drama, and Bullying

Cathy thought about her friends. There are some she loves and trusts and others who constantly gossip and create conflict. One is an attention seeker and will do anything to get attention. Another is so desperate for popularity that she goes against her values and does things because everyone else is doing it. Cathy realized she needed to be more careful with choosing her friends.

She remembered what Coach told her earlier, "There are friends, and there are acquaintances. There's a difference between the two. An acquaintance is someone you know but may not be close friends with. You may share a class or group with them without knowing their details. A friend is someone you care about and connect with. You spend time with friends and share secrets with them. Take a look at your friends. Who are they? What do they stand for? You will be judged by the people you hang around. Make sure your friends add value to your life. It is *also important to make sure you add value to them. People are like math; they add to you, subtract from you, divide you, or cause you to multiply. If you want great friends, you must also be a great friend."*

Chapter 7: Butterfly Harmony

Relationship Mathematics

Everyone needs a good friend. Your friends are a big part of your life. They are like the beautiful blossoms on a flower. The world would be a lonely place without friends. They add joy and excitement to your life. You can count on them when you need them. If you have one good friend, you are fortunate.

Friendships are a lot like mathematics. Coach reminded us that friends would add to you, subtract from you, multiply, or divide you. Your friends can put you in a positive or negative situation. Good friends motivate you to be your best self, encourage you, and celebrate your accomplishments. True friends are not haters. Please look at the chart below. Where do your friends fit?

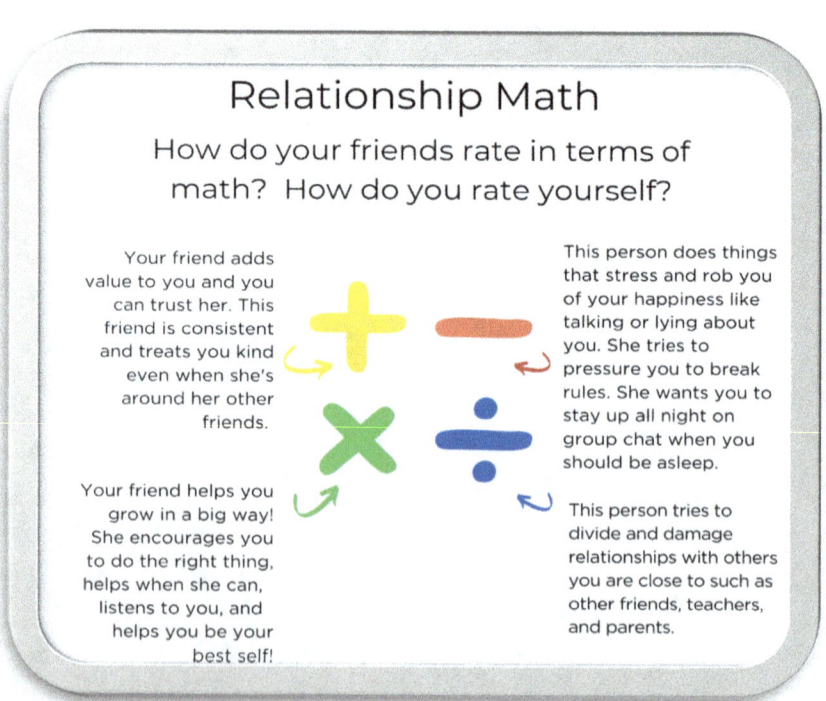

Count the Cost

If you hang out with friends who make poor decisions, you could face the same consequences as them, even if you're innocent. Javon, a well-behaved student, had been warned by his mother to stay away from a group of friends known for their negative influence. He didn't listen to his mother's advice. One day, he ended up taking a ride with them, unaware of their plan to rob a store. Although Javon did not take part in the robbery, he was still arrested for being present during the crime. This situation proves that friends can influence your life, for better or worse. Parents often have an insight and a good sense about which friends might positively or negatively impact you. This is the reason it is important to listen to their advice.

Sometimes you may need to remove someone from your circle. For instance, there's Tonya, your friend since 1st grade. She's always in drama, spreading rumors, and posting disrespectful things on social media. Tonya's behavior in school isn't great either, and she makes bad choices like stealing and lying. Despite talking to her about changing, she doesn't seem to care. It's like she's subtracting and dividing at the same time.

If you find yourself in a similar situation, you may need to "lose" your friend until she changes. If she doesn't change her behavior, you have to make a change to protect your peace and reputation. A reputation is made up of beliefs that others have about you and your character. If you need to pull away from a friend, do it gracefully and respectfully. You might say, *"I don't like it when you spread rumors and gossip about others."* You can limit the conversations with her. You don't have to be mean, but you can handle her differently. See the friendship for what it is and count the cost.

Every person has positive traits as well as flaws. Friends have good days and bad days, just as you have good and bad days. When you think about the words, *"good friend"* what comes to mind? Write your answers below.

_____

_____

_____

_____

12 Keys to a Good Friendship

Good friendships are built on trust, kindness, and respect. Building friendships is an ongoing process. It takes time, patience, and understanding. Here are key traits of good friendships:

Key 1: Trust - Trust is the foundation of strong friendships. You should be able to confide in your friends and trust them to keep secrets and support you.

Key 2: Empathy - Empathy is the ability to put yourself in your friend's shoes and feel her experience. It involves listening and offering support during tough times.

Key 3: Listening - Do you listen when your friend talks, or are you focused on what you will say next? Listening involves being quiet and letting someone talk and finish.

Key 4: Honesty - Good friends tell the truth in a loving way, even when the truth is difficult to hear. Honesty builds trust and helps resolve conflicts.

Key 5: Respect - Friends respect each other's values, feelings, thoughts, and uniqueness. They value you although they don't always agree with you. They accept you instead of trying to change you.

Key 6: Kindness - Kindness means being thoughtful and considerate of your friends. Kindness strengthens friendships.

Chapter 7: Butterfly Harmony

 **Key 7: Supportiveness** - Friends support each other's goals, celebrate each other's accomplishments, and provide encouragement when there is a challenge.

 **Key 8: Equality** - Equality happens when friends add to the relationship in similar ways. It's not one-sided. It is not all about you or your friend.

 **Key 9: Apologizing and Forgiving** - Friends apologize when they are wrong. Many apologize by saying, "I'm sorry." Express what you are apologizing for. Friends forgive. We all make mistakes!

 **Key 10: Inclusion** - Inclusion means involving your friends in your activities. Do you include your friend in activities when other girls are around?

 **Key 11: Fun** - Friendship is enjoyable when you laugh and have fun. Good friends have fun with one another.

 **Key 12: Communication** - Communication is important in every friendship! Friends freely express their needs, feelings, and concerns.

How to Handle Girl Drama

At some point, every girl will have to deal with some form of girl drama. You can choose how you will handle it. Some girls become very emotional and find it overwhelming, while others refuse to let the drama affect them deeply. How do you manage such situations?

Evolved Girl, Anyielle, a 5th grader, offered her advice about how to handle girl drama.

Chapter 7: Butterfly Harmony

Keep it Moving

"When girls tell me that someone said something about me, it does not upset me. I tell them I don't care in a nice way. It does not matter how they feel about me. I know how I feel about me. I don't ask questions or stick around to get more information. I just keep it moving and walk past the girls. When I see that gossip or rumors are starting, I still keep it moving. I feel that you have to know when to walk on."

Anyielle offered good advice! Know when to move on. There are some students who make it their business to push your buttons so that you can react. Don't allow the drama to pull you in and change your personality. Here are other tips for managing girl drama:

1. Don't spread rumors or gossip. A rumor is something you hear but you do not know whether or not it's true.

2. Don't tell girls what others say about them. This causes unnecessary hurt and fights. Pay attention to how many times you catch yourself saying, "she said" or "he said."

3. Don't say anything behind a girl's back that you wouldn't want to say to her.

4. Treat other girls the way you want to be treated. There is a principle called sowing and reaping. Whatever you plant or give out, will come back to you!

5. Build girls up instead of tearing them down. You don't know their stories. Some of them go through horrible things at home that you can't imagine. There are some who don't

have a home to call their own; they are living in a car or motel because they are homeless.

Grade Your Friends

Now that you have learned the keys to building strong friendships, pause for a moment and complete the inventory below by answering "yes" or "no." As you reflect on the questions, you will gain a better understanding of your friendships and see how they measure up.

MY FRIENDS: INVENTORY

- Is it easy to talk and express your feelings to your friend? _____
- Does your friend listen to you and understand you? _____
- Can you trust her? _____
- Does your friend encourage you? _____
- Is your friend happy when you accomplish something? _____

If you answered "yes" to most or all of these questions, your friend is fantastic and she adds value to you.

- Does she gossip or instigate? _____
- Does she talk about other people's business? _____
- Does she create unnecessary drama? _____
- Does her name come up when there is mess? _____
- Does she try to control your friendships or tell you who you should and should not be friends with? _____

Be careful if you answered "yes" to most or all of these questions. This friend subtracts from you and creates division!

Chapter 7: Butterfly Harmony

As you worked through those questions, what stood out to you? How do your friends measure up? Now, it is time to evaluate yourself as a friend. It is important to be the kind of friend to others that you would expect.

ME, AS A FRIEND: INVENTORY

- I could easily be a best friend to a girl like me. _____
- I solve more problems than I create. _____
- I encourage and support my friends when they are having a tough time. _____
- My friend can trust me with her secrets. _____

If you answered "yes" to most or all of these questions, you are a trusted friend!

- I am quick to gossip or say, "She said / he said." _____
- I have a hard time keeping secrets. *(Note: It may be necessary to break the confidence of a friend for her safety or others. If she threatens to harm herself or others, encourage her to talk to a trusted adult. If she doesn't, you may have to tell a trusted adult to get the support and safety she needs).*
- I often create problems and conflicts____
- I tell my friends who they should be friends with. _____
- I am always in the middle of drama. _____

What kind of friend are you? If you answered "yes" to most or all of these questions, please be willing to change your behavior. It's time to evolve!

The Big Bad Wolf: The Bully

Do you remember the story of the three little pigs? They spent most of their time running away from the big bad wolf who threatened to harm them. For the little pigs, life was filled with fear and anxiety. However, by the end of the story, the wolf found himself in a hot mess! Bullying, puts everyone involved in a bad situation.

Let's be clear about what bullying is. Often, a student reports that someone is bullying her only to find out that it is not bullying. So, what are examples of bullying?

- Teasing
- Name-calling
- Spreading rumors or sharing secrets about someone
- Threatening to harm someone
- Isolating and excluding (telling other girls not to talk to or hang around someone)
- Taking something from someone (candy, snacks, pencils, lunch, and clothes)
- Hitting, touching, or pushing
- Staring (looking) at someone with the intention of trying to scare her
- Using technology (phone, tablet, social media) to threaten someone or talk mean to them. This type of bullying is called "cyberbullying."

Chapter 7: Butterfly Harmony

In my experience as a counselor, I've noticed that students who bully others often have their own problems. Many bullies feel angry and sad because of issues in their lives they can't fix. They hurt inside and don't know how to handle these feelings. Often, kids bully at school because they're bullied at home. They target classmates that they feel are weak.

Bullies tend to believe putting others down makes them more powerful. If you often find yourself teasing, hitting, being rude, or trying to scare people, it's wise to talk to a school counselor. It's important to learn how to manage your actions and feelings and understand why you act this way. No one wants to be friends with someone who bullies others. If you act like the big bad wolf, you won't have lasting friendships. Always remember to treat people the way you want someone to treat your younger brother or sister. How would you feel if someone teased, hit, or took something from them? You wouldn't be happy.

Mallory's Story

Mallory is an awesome, thoughtful, and well-mannered middle-school student. She has a beautiful personality that is going to take her very far. She dealt with bullies for a while. Let's learn about Mallory and her journey with Big Bad Wolves.

Evolved Girl

"When I was in elementary school, there were a couple of girls who bullied me. I wanted to be their friend so much, but they would only act like my friends when they wanted something from me. The rest of the time, they called me names, made fun of me, and left me out. I was confused and hurt. Because I wanted to be friends with them, I let them treat me this way. I thought that letting them treat me however they wanted would make them want to be my friends. What it really did was make me feel anxious and bad about myself all the time. It was like I couldn't see the good in myself anymore. I only saw the things that they made fun of as being true. Then, one day, a real friend stood up for me. We were on the playground when she heard them speak to me in an ugly way. She said, "You can treat Mallory like you treat the rest of us, or you can leave!" The bullies backed down. Even though my mom and my counselor had told me that standing up to them would make the situation better, I didn't believe it until I saw it happen. Having a real friend show me how to be assertive helped me to start believing that I could be assertive too! Now I have more confidence, and I know that when others say mean things about me that doesn't mean they are true. I also know that standing up for myself isn't disrespectful or unkind."

Chapter 7: Butterfly Harmony

Now, Mallory uses her voice and does not allow other students to mistreat her. Her good friend helped her realize that she did not have to be a victim to bullying and disrespect.

> ### What Would You Do?
>
> A new student just joined your classroom. She seems a little shy. She is nervous about being in a new school. What can you do to help her feel welcome?

Remember this…

Everyone needs a caring and loving friend. Choose good friends. More important, choose to be a good friend. Good friends are more valuable than precious gems.

CHAPTER 8: UNFOLD YOUR FUTURE WINGS
– Exploring Careers

As Cathy and her friends flew around the beautiful flowers, she thought about Coach. She wondered how she became such a good Butterfly Counselor. Coach had helped her and her friends evolve. Cathy and her friends flew until they found Coach relaxing on a lavender flower. When she saw Coach, she asked with excitement, "Do you have a second to chat?" Coach nodded in agreement. "Coach, how did you know which career to choose when you were my age? Is it too early for me to think about my career and purpose?"

Coach gently responded, "Cathy, there are always clues that answer your questions. You have talent and skills that you are using right now. Everyone has a genius within. Some are good at writing, solving math, or fixing things. Others are awesome athletes, teachers, or great communicators (and may get in trouble for talking). My brother knew at a young age that he would be a teacher. My aunt knew she wanted to be a doctor at your age. In 4th grade, my classmates called me 'Counselor' *because I gave them advice and helped solve their problems. If you are trying to figure out what you do well, ask your parents, family, teachers, and friends. They will help you with your discovery. Others may see your talent when you don't recognize it. A combination of your talent, skills, and personality will point you to the best career choice."*

Recognize Your Superpowers!

There is a genius within you! A genius has exceptional talent, ability, or insight in a certain area. These talents, abilities, and special skills make up your superpower! Everyone has a superpower or an area where they shine.

Have you ever wondered about your future career? Career fairs at school are a great way to help students discover their interests and talents. If you start this process of self-discovery now, it will guide your decisions about your future career. This understanding allows you to select classes and extracurricular activities that align with your strengths. For example, if you have a passion for music, you might choose to take music classes or join the school band or orchestra. If you excel in math and science, you may find yourself drawn to STEM (Science, Technology, Engineering, and Math) classes and clubs.

Remember, your talents may differ from those of your friends or siblings. If you do not enjoy music, don't feel pressured to join the chorus simply because your friend did. Choose classes that highlight your strengths and interests, rather than ones you dislike.

Your Superpower Shapes Your Future

Understanding your superpower will also help you choose your first job and career as an adult. Many students wait until they are in high school to explore careers. Now is the time to explore. You might ask, "What is a career?"

> **career**
>
> the job, trade, or profession that one is trained to do; the job that you do for a living to make money.

A career is a profession, job, or trade you've trained for to make money and take care of your responsibilities.

Your education, talents, and experiences prepare you for a career. You will feel wingless if you don't see where you are going and how you will get there. It is not necessary to choose a career now, but now is the time to begin exploring. Some girls already know what they want to do as adults. This section helps create awareness about yourself and career options so that you can think about your future.

You can learn more about careers through career guidance programs and assessments (such as Kuder or Naviance) at your school. Visit with your school counselor to get more information about career resources. As you explore, keep in mind that a career is not the same as a hobby. A hobby is something that you do for fun. It might be fishing, singing, planting a garden, walking the dog, or baking cookies for your family. A career is an assignment that you get paid and trained to do. Some hobbies can become careers.

Life After School

"Make good grades so that you can go to college" are the words preached to students by parents and teachers. Every student should have a plan for success after high school. But here's the truth: College alone does not guarantee success. Some college graduates are successful, while some are unemployed or unhappy because they are doing jobs they don't like. Some trade school graduates make more money than college graduates. I'm telling you this so that you know your "what and why." A company will not hire you just because you have a degree or know information. You get hired because you have a skill they need. As you learn more about yourself, you will understand the best path. Here are some options to consider after high school:

College or University: A college or university is a big school that offers a program that leads to a Bachelor's degree. Students can also earn Master's and Doctorate degrees later. Students can decide what they want to learn. People attend a university to become teachers, doctors, scientists, and more. Universities have huge libraries with thousands of books. The teachers at the university are called professors. They are experts in what they teach. Some professors write their own textbooks.

When I ask students what they plan to do after high school, many say, "I'm going to college." They usually don't say why they are going or what they want to become. College is a place that prepares you to *be* and *do*. It is the beginning of a journey, not the end. What do you plan to do with the education that you get? What will you become after you receive your college degree?

If you're unsure about your reason for attending college, you might end up changing your major many times. This will cost your parents or yourself more money while you try to figure things out. Know what you want to do before you show up. When I worked at a university, I met many students who were happy, excited, and on track for success. But, some students didn't have a clue why they were there. They wandered like lost puppies.

College offers a fun and exciting experience! It's a place where you'll make friends and form lasting relationships. Many students enjoy living on campus in dormitories, which offers some independence. With this increased freedom comes the need for greater discipline. Professors, unlike high school teachers, expect you to manage your responsibilities independently. They won't remind you about assignment deadlines or contact your parents if you're failing. Making an effort to get to know your professors can be very helpful; they can assist you in your job search or provide awesome recommendation letters.

> CHOOSING A COLLEGE: If your career choice requires a 4-year college degree or higher, you can research with the end in mind. Go online and explore a university you are interested in. Go to Admissions area and find the program that interests you. Research the classes the students must take while they are there. You can also learn the high school requirements you need to get in. This research helps you select courses in high school.

Community College: Community colleges offer two-year degree programs or certifications. It can prepare you for a job or a transfer to a four-year college. I attended a community college before transferring to a 4-year college.

Trade or Technical School: These schools provide training in plumbing, electrical work, culinary arts, cosmetology, and more. This training leads to specific job opportunities. Have you ever watched chefs on Food Network? Many of them attended a culinary arts school. If you have gone to a hair salon or barber shop, a professional who attended a trade school serviced you.

Workforce: Some students get a job directly after high school and find entry-level jobs that offer opportunities for growth and advancement.

Military Service: Some graduates may choose to join the military. It offers training, career development, and benefits. It can be a way to serve your country and gain valuable skills.

Entrepreneurship: An entrepreneur is a person who owns a business. Starting a business requires you to have a product or service, focus, a plan, and dedication.

Don't Let Anyone Steal Your Shine!

You are destined for success! Don't underestimate yourself because of your race, gender, or background. Don't let anyone else count you out or tell you what you can or cannot achieve. A physician friend shared her experience with one of the Evolved Girls, encouraging her to pursue her dreams.

When Dr. Johnson was a school girl, she told her school counselor that she wanted to be a doctor, the counselor told her she couldn't and wouldn't become a doctor! The counselor certainly did not believe in her, even though she was a very smart, respectful student who made excellent grades. She knew the counselor discouraged and discriminated against her because of her race. This still happens today! Suppose Dr. Johnson allowed that counselor to steal her dream?

You might have an experience where a teacher, counselor, or professional tries to discriminate against you and discourage you because of their small mindset. Not all teachers and school professionals are fair. Some have their own issues and biases that they bring to school with them. Be wise enough to know when someone is trying to rob your dream or steal your shine!

Now, let's have a moment of truth. To become a medical doctor, you must do well in science and math and pass advanced classes. If you want to be a doctor and you have consistently failed math and science, it is unlikely that you will meet the requirements. In this case, someone should tell you it will only happen if you turn your grades around.

Self- Discovery

It is time for self-discovery. You learned about your superpowers, intelligence, and strengths. Pause for a moment to get in touch with yourself. Answer the questions below:

1. What is your favorite class? Why? Which classes do you make the best grade(s) in?

_____

_____

_____

2. What are your favorite activities? (This does not have to be school-related.)

_____

_____

_____

3. Which of these do you prefer? (Circle the ones that you enjoy.)

- Creating things (food, art, designing clothing, music)
- Helping people
- Teaching others how to do something
- Talking
- Expressing yourself through writing
- Working with technology
- Connecting with animals

The information you just learned will guide your decisions about future classes and extracurricular activities.

Shadowing and Interviewing

Do you have a clear idea of the career path you want to pursue? If so, consider asking your parents if they know anyone working in that field who you could interview. This conversation could provide valuable insights into the necessary qualifications and the work environment. You might even have the opportunity to shadow this person at their job. If visiting the workplace isn't possible, prepare questions such as, "What classes should I take to prepare for this job? What skills are important? What do you enjoy or find challenging about your work? How can I start preparing now? Which schools or programs would you recommend?" Also, your school's career fair can be a great place to meet professionals and ask these questions. With a wide range of careers available, exploring the Career Clusters can help you learn more about various career options.

The 16 National Career Clusters®

The National Career Clusters® Framework (www.careertech.org) provides a structure for organizing career and technical education (CTE) programs through learning and comprehensive programs of study. The clusters represent more than 79 Career Pathways to help students navigate their way to great success in college and careers.

Agriculture, Food & Natural Resources
production, processing, marketing, distribution, financing, and development of agricultural commodities and resources

Hospitality & Tourism
management, marketing, and operations of restaurants and other food services, lodging, attractions, recreation events and travel related services

Architecture & Construction
designing, planning, managing, building and maintaining the built environment

Human Services
providing family and human services such as counseling, mental health services, family and community services, personal care, and consumer services

Arts, A/V Technology & Communications
designing, producing, exhibiting, performing, writing, and publishing multimedia

Information Technology
designing, developing, supporting and managing hardware, software, multimedia and systems integration services

Business Management & Administration
planning, organizing, directing and evaluating business functions essential to efficient and productive business operations

Law, Public Safety, Corrections & Security
planning, managing, and providing legal, public safety, protective services and homeland security

Education & Training
planning, managing and providing education and training services and related learning support services

Manufacturing
planning, managing and performing the processing of materials into intermediate or final products and related professional and technical support activities

Finance
planning, services for financial and investment planning, banking, insurance, and business financial management

Marketing
promoting and selling goods and services

Government & Public Administration
planning and performing government functions at the local, state and federal levels

Science, Technology, Engineering & Mathematics
planning, managing and providing scientific research and professional and technical services related S.T.E.M.

Health Sciences
planning, managing, and providing therapeutic services, diagnostic services, health informatics, support services, and biotechnology research and development

Transportation, Distribution & Logistics
planning, management, and movement of people, materials, and goods by road, pipeline, air, rail and water and related professional support services

Chapter 8: Unfold Your Future Wings

CAREER AWARENESS WORKSHEET

1. Which three career clusters excite you the most?

_____

_____

_____

2. What do you picture yourself doing to make a living when you become an adult?

_____

_____

_____

3. *Here's your homework*. Choose the career you are most interested in and research the following:

  a. Education Requirements: Do you have to attend college or trade school?

  b. High School Requirements: Are there classes you can take in high school to prepare you or help you learn more about your career choice?

  c. Average Salary: You can ask Google what the average salary is. You can also visit the [Department of Labor website](#) to learn more about career salaries.

  d. Work Environment. What is the work environment like in this career? What type of environment do you like?

e. School Options: What schools can you attend to get the training for this career?

f. Internship Requirement: Will you have to do an internship while you are learning?

What Would You Do?

You want to be a school principal when you grow up. You often dream about being a school principal. How will you get more information about becoming a principal?

Remember this...

You now have a head start toward your career! Be proactive. Being proactive means that you will take action and responsibility for your choices, starting now. You don't have to wait to figure things out. You will be successful in your career! Prepare for your future now. Develop the habits, mindset, and attitude that will unlock doors for you. Expect success in your career. Most importantly, choose a career that you love!

CHAPTER 9: BRAVE WINGS — Standing Tall Against Peer Pressure

"Coach, so many students at Butterfly Academy give in to peer pressure," Cathy said. Coach cleared her throat and began, "Many students want to be liked. They often go out of their way to gain the approval and acceptance of others. What students don't realize is that others respect them more when they have the courage to be themselves. There is good peer pressure and bad peer pressure. Good peer pressure inspires you to improve yourself. Bad peer pressure leads you to make decisions you'll regret or that harm you or others. Whenever you're about to make a decision, think about its consequences on your life. Some decisions can affect you for the rest of your life." Cathy reflected on Coach's words. She realized she had given in to peer pressure significantly. She promised herself that she would no longer let others control her life or influence her negatively.

What is Peer Pressure?

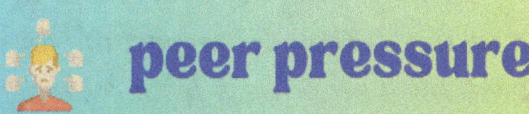

(1) influence from the members of your peer group; (2) the pressure of feeling and thinking that you need to do something so that you will be accepted by your peer group.

Peer pressure is real! Many students make decisions about what to wear and how to act, based on peer pressure. If you do something because others are doing it, you're giving in to peer pressure. Don't allow other people to set the rules for you. Yes, certain fashions, technology, behaviors, and apps are popular. But be clear about why you are doing something.

There is a lot of peer pressure about clothing, especially shoes. Some students tease others because they don't wear designer shoes that others are wearing. What does it prove if you wear shoes that cost $300, but have low grades because you don't work hard? What's the point if you wear these shoes but have a bad attitude? When you take the shoes off, you are still you. Clothes should never mean more than your attitude or grades.

Confessions of a Young Girl

These are the words of a girl who struggled with peer pressure. She grew tired of allowing others to influence her.

"I want to be accepted and liked. But I will not sink my ship to win acceptance from others. I will not allow them to make me into a person that I am not. They will respect me for who I am. If I follow the crowd, I will never be a leader. Leaders are not afraid to be different. If I follow anyone, it will be a person who is leading me in a good direction."

Identifying Areas of Peer Pressure

Many students feel they have to prove something to their friends. This feeling and belief can cause students to make choices or have behavior they would not ordinarily have made. Peer pressure can cause students to be someone else, instead of being themselves.

PEER PRESSURE INVENTORY

1. What are some areas where you or other students face peer pressure? (Write them below.)

   _____
   _____
   _____

2. Where or who is your peer pressure coming from?

_____

_____

_____

3. How are you handling the pressure in your life?
_____
_____
_____
_____

4. Is peer pressure stressing you out?
_____
_____
_____

5. Who can you talk to when you feel pressured?
_____
_____
_____

6. Are you willing to set boundaries?
_____
_____
_____

Chapter 9: Brave Wings

How to Manage Peer Pressure

Peer pressure is negative or positive. If your sister convinces you to make the honor roll so that your parents take a family trip to Disney World, this is an example of good peer pressure. If your friend tries to influence you to start vaping, this is an example of negative peer pressure. Here are some ways that you can handle or manage peer pressure:

1. ***Think about the consequences.*** When you feel pressured to do something, ask yourself, "What are the consequences? How will this affect me, my friends, parents, or teachers?" Peer pressure is also harmful to parents. Be thoughtful of your family as you navigate through peer pressure. It costs money to keep up with your peers. I have seen students ask parents for phones, electronics, or clothes they couldn't afford. A student once told me that their electricity was cut off because their parents purchased electronic devices instead of paying the electric bill. So, they lived in darkness for a while. This is an example of the student and parent giving in to peer pressure. Don't create hardships for your family to prove a point to someone who doesn't care.

2. ***Determine why you are doing it.*** When you make a decision, know why you are doing it. Are you doing it because it's something you want or need? Are you trying to impress someone?

3. ***Pay attention to your gut!*** Sometimes you will have a nagging feeling that you shouldn't do something. You'll get

knots in your stomach. *You won't always want to follow the crowd.* Pay attention to the warning signs.

4. ***Have the strength to set boundaries and say "no."*** Others will respect you when you set the necessary limits. You don't have to be a *yes* girl to win friends and acceptance.

What Would You Do?

You don't feel very good about yourself. Payton and Amber wear designer clothes every day. They have brand name shoes and purses. They have the latest model of the iPhone. The other girls flock to them because they always look good. Your parents won't buy you expensive clothes and electronics because they are saving money for a new home. Does this make Payton and Amber better than you? What can you tell yourself to change how you feel about this?

Remember this...

Peer pressure does not have to be stressful. You have the power to choose what is best for you. Use your power! You've had it all along. From this day forward, promise yourself that you will be you and march to your own beat even if no one else hears it! When you know your value, you won't try to win the approval of others.

CHAPTER 10: LOVE YOUR WINGS – A Journey to Self-Care

Cathy flew to Butterfly Academy. She was not herself this week. She felt anxious and annoyed by small things. She also noticed that she made more mistakes than usual. She couldn't figure out why she felt out of sorts. Coach was waiting for her when she landed on her flower petal. "Hello, Coach," Cathy said faintly. Coach responded, "How are you doing and feeling today? You seem a little down." Cathy answered, "I'm not sure why. I wish this feeling would disappear; I don't feel motivated. I don't want to be here today. Sometimes I have so many emotions I am dealing with." Coach asked, "Cathy, what time do you go to bed?" As Cathy prepared to answer, she put her head down. "Hmmm. Well, I've been going to bed pretty late. My friends and I have a group chat and sometimes talk through the night. Sometimes, I play games or watch videos on my wing phone," she said softly. Coach replied, "There it is. You are not practicing self-care. Cathy, the amount of sleep you get or don't get affects how you think, act, feel, and function. Many students feel the same way you do, but they don't know why. Now is a good time to learn how to care for your mind, body, and spirit. There are things your parents can *do to support you, but you also have to do some things independently."* Cathy recognized she had the power to change how she was feeling.

Chapter 10: Love Your Wings

Do you remember when you played with dolls? You cared for them and made sure they had everything they needed to feel loved. You may have given your doll a name, changed her clothes and put her to bed. Have you stopped to wonder if you are caring for yourself the same way?

As you grow, learn how to take care of yourself so you can live your best life. You are made up of physical and non-physical matter, which includes your mind, body, and spirit. Evolved Girls pay attention to the: *body* (hygiene, diet, and sleep), *emotions* (feelings and heart), and *mind* (thoughts).

I have a secret to tell you; the things you do daily affect your emotions, behavior, health and ability to focus in school. You will function at your best when you understand how to care for yourself! Sleep deprivation, anxiety, depression, drugs, and relationships are some of the issues that affect tweens and teens.

Sleep Deprivation

One way that students harm themselves is through a lack of sleep. That's right! Young students are experiencing sleep deprivation more than ever. Sleep deprivation means your body is not getting the amount of sleep needed to function. You might not think this is a big deal, but it is! Your body needs 8 or 10 hours of sleep. Even if you are not sleepy at night, you need rest. Here's why:

According to the National Institute of Health, sleep promotes healthy brain function. It helps with learning and forming your memory. Also, while you sleep, your body releases hormones that repair cells and control the body's use of energy. Sleep helps with weight control and fighting germs (because it boosts your immune system).

Symptoms of Sleep Deprivation

Sleep deprivation affects your well-being. You or your parents may overlook sleep deprivation symptoms and assume it's something else. Difficulty focusing at school might be due to lack of sleep. According to the Cleveland Clinic, these are the symptoms of sleep deprivation:

- Irritability;
- Trouble thinking, concentrating, and remembering;
- Mood changes (increased anxiety, depression, and quick temper);
- Hallucinations (seeing, hearing, smelling, and feeling things that seem real, but are not real);
- Falling asleep in class;
- Uncontrollable eye movements (nystagmus);
- Fatigue (being tired all the time);
- Higher risk of diabetes and heart problems;
- Slowed reaction times;

Chapter 10: Love Your Wings

- Trouble speaking clearly; and
- Headaches.

If you experience any of these symptoms, you may be sleep-deprived. Here are a few ideas to help you get on track with your sleep:

- 😴 Turn the cell phone or tablet off at a certain time and go to bed. Being up all night is not cool. It will create mental health and physical problems. Your mind and health are more important than staying up.

- 😴 If you don't have a bedtime, set one for yourself. For sure, your body should be in bed by 9 on a school night. This means that you will have to set a boundary with others.

> **Self-care is not a selfish act; it is a self-full act. When you care for yourself, you are treating yourself like the gift that you are. Value your body and mind and make yourself a priority.**

Managing Anxiety

Academic pressures, social issues, and personal challenges can cause anxiety. Here are some tips to deal with anxiety:

1. Talk to someone you trust, such as your parents or school counselor (especially your parents). Sharing your feelings can make you feel better and less alone. Let your parents know if you need to speak to a therapist

or doctor. Your parent has to give permission to help you because you are a minor.

2. Practice deep breathing when you start to feel anxious. Inhale slowly through your nose for a count of four, hold for a count of four, and then exhale slowly through your mouth for a count of four. Repeat this a few times to calm yourself down. Deep breathing allows more air to flow into your body, which can calm your nerves and reduce stress and anxiety.

3. Pay attention to the triggers. A trigger is a situation, thought, or action that causes certain responses or feelings.

4. Have positive self-talk. Replace negative thoughts with positive ones. When you think something negative like "I can't do this," change it to "I can do this. I'll give it my all."

5. Exercise and play. Physical activities like walking, biking, and sports can reduce anxiety and depression.

6. Limit screen time. Monitor the amount of the time you spend online, especially on social media. Comparing yourself to others on social media can create feelings of "not being enough." If you experience anxiety after going on social media, avoid it. Not everyone can handle social media.

7. Get enough sleep. Lack of sleep can make anxiety and depression worse.

8. Break tasks into small steps if you're overwhelmed with a big project or homework so that it is less stressful.

Remember, it's normal to feel anxious at times. You're not alone. With practice and support, you can manage your anxiety and feel better.

Handling Depression

Sometimes students feel depressed, especially if they are trying to cope with the death of a loved one, a parent who is ill, a family crisis, or the death of a pet. These are not the only reasons that students may feel depressed. If you feel depressed, refer to the tips listed in the *Managing Anxiety* section and combine them with these tips:

- **Try to figure out why and when you started to feel depressed.** This can help you create a plan to overcome or manage depression. If you are depressed now, it doesn't mean you will always be depressed!

- **Express your feelings.** Art, music, and journaling can be helpful tools to deal with your feelings. The Evolved Girl Journal is available to help you track and express your feelings. This journal also the benefits of journaling.

- **Stay connected to people who care about you.** Try to maintain your connections with friends and family, even if you don't feel like talking or being around them. Shutting people out of your life makes you feel lonely and that will make you feel worse. Don't shut people out!

- **Reach out to a trusted adult for help and support.** You don't have to go through this alone. People care about you and want to help you feel better. Depression is a treatable condition. With the right help, you can find your way towards a brighter future.

Self-Care Before and During Your Period

Menstruation is a natural and normal part of life for girls and women. The average age that girls get their period is twelve, but it can be sooner or later. Since you will have a period (menstruation) for a long time, it is important to know how to care for yourself before and during your period.

Coping with Pre-Menstrual Syndrome (PMS)

How many times have you heard your mother, sister, or friend say, "I'm PMS-ing"? Emotions can become a little sensitive just before your period starts. PMS (Premenstrual Syndrome) refers to the emotional and physical symptoms that occur before or during a period. These symptoms can range from sadness, breast tenderness, fatigue, mood swings, anxiety, bloating, and acne. Usually, these symptoms will leave after the first few days of the period.

Since you know that you are going to be very emotional the week before your period, give yourself some grace if you find yourself crying for no reason. Avoid heated discussions especially if you know that your emotions are running the show. If you feel sad and out of control, it may be helpful to let your parents or family members know what's going on so they can support you or stay out of your way! Try not to take things too personally during PMS week.

Handling Your Period

The Center for Disease Control (CDC) along with other health organizations provide tips on how to take care of your hygiene during your period. Good hygiene during your period can help prevent infections, reduce odors, and keep you comfortable. Here are a few tips:

- **Keep your hands clean.** Wash your hands after using the restroom and before using a pad or tampon.

- **Choose products carefully:** It may be best to use unscented pads, tampons and toilet paper. Though they smell good, the fragrance in them can irritate your skin and cause a rash.

- **Avoid the odor:** As blood leaves your body, it mixes with bacteria which produces an odor. According to data and research, some report that period blood smells fishy, especially after it dries. The best way to avoid odor is to change your pad regularly and keep your genital area clean. One of the ways to keep your genital area clean is to use genital wipes to clean yourself when you use the bathroom and change your pad. Just be sure you are using the proper wipes! You should not use regular disinfectant wipes.

- **Change your pad or tampon:** Change sanitary pads every 3-4 hours no matter how light the flow. Change them more frequently if your period is heavy. According to Tampax, you should change tampons every 4 to 6 hours. The Cleveland Clinic says that you risk Toxic Shock Syndrome if you leave a tampon in for longer than 8 hours.

- **Wrap your pad**: Discard used pads properly by first wrapping them with toilet paper before putting them in the trash. No one wants to see a bloody pad in the trash can. Do not flush pads down the toilet because it can clog the toilet and cause it to back up and overflow.

- **Choose the right clothes:** Wear lightweight, breathable clothing (such as cotton underwear). Tight fabrics can trap moisture and heat, which allows germs to thrive.

- **Drink enough liquids.** This can help wash out your urinary tract and help prevent infections, like vaginal candidiasis.

Chapter 10: Love Your Wings

You Have a Voice

Using your voice is an example of self-care. When you use your voice, it not only impacts you, it impacts others as well. When you use your voice, you are:

- **Expressing Your Feelings and Thoughts:** You share what's on your mind and what's in your heart.

- **Guiding and Inspiring Others**: As a leader, you use your voice to inspire, teach, and encourage others. Others are looking to you because you are a role model. If you are the Class President or Hall Monitor, you will use your voice to lead.

- **Speaking Up About Something Important to You:** Here's an example–You really care about keeping your classroom clean. You frequently see empty potato chip bags and candy wrappers on the floor. If you nicely encourage students to put their empty candy wrappers in the trash can, you are using your voice to encourage cleanliness.

- **Handling Unacceptable Behavior:** If you see someone with inappropriate behavior, you might speak up and let the person know it's not okay. You may have to also report this behavior to a leader so that it can be addressed. Another word for speaking up is *advocating*. Here is a true story and example of about Dylan advocating for himself and others.

> *Dylan, a special-needs young adult, participates in a community program daily. One day, the Program Coordinator, called the students an inappropriate and racially offensive name. Dylan reported this incident to the supervisor. As a consequence, the Coordinator was sent home, and an investigation was started. Dylan's decision to speak up brought much-needed attention to the offensive behavior. Although it was uncomfortable for him to report this, his courage helped to raise awareness and protect other students from similar disrespect. His actions sent a clear message that such behavior was unacceptable. In response, the management team meetings with teachers and coordinators to remind them of the expectations and the consequences of failing to meet these expectations.*

Protect Yourself

Fortunately, Dylan did not suffer in silence. He used his voice to bring about change. Young girls face many issues and sometimes suffer in silence. Unfortunately, many girls have experienced abuse and neglect. Some are being abused or neglected at home by family members. You have the right to be heard and protected if you are being mistreated, bullied, or harmed. There are people available to help.

Many assume that they are stuck with no way of changing. Your counselor can assist and provide you with resources. Know this: if you go to your counselor for help, his or her focus is to support you and help you get the needed resources. If you tell your counselor you are being abused, the counselor may report this to a child protective agency. If your counselor knows about abuse and doesn't report it, she may lose her job and professional license. If you are in this situation and feel afraid to talk to someone at school, you might talk to a family member or someone you trust. The goal is to stop the abuse.

Some students may say things like, "Snitches get stitches or land in ditches." Sometimes bullies or people who hurt others make threats so that a person does not tell. That's a game that many play because they fear the consequences. You can't protect the bully and yourself. If you remain quiet when someone harms you, you are giving that person the permission to keep hurting you!

What's in Your Mouth?

Your diet plays a crucial role in your overall well-being. Treating your body right by consuming the right kinds of foods and drinks can have a significant impact on how you feel and behave. For example, consuming too much caffeine can lead to feelings of anxiety and jitteriness. Caffeine is commonly found in beverages such as Coke, Pepsi, tea, coffee, and energy drinks like Red Bull, and it can also increase your heart rate.

High sugar intake is another dietary concern. According to Healthline, excessive sugar consumption can cause acne, weight gain, and type 2 diabetes, which increases the risk of various medical conditions. Research indicates that a high-sugar diet can cause memory issues, learning difficulties, and emotional disorders, including anxiety and depression. It's important to remember that many foods serve beneficial purposes and can help you maintain good health. To improve your diet, consider drinking more water, eating more green vegetables, and reducing your sugar consumption.

Vaping and Drug Use

Drug use and vaping is a big problem among school-age students. Vaping and drug use have serious consequences on health and well-being. Drug use affects your brain development, academic performance, and social life. Drugs also create legal consequences that can cause jail time, fines, and probation. Vaping can lead to respiratory issues, heart problems, and lung injuries.

Marijuana is a popular drug. THC is the chemical in marijuana that causes the high. It can lead to addiction, mental illness, violence, crime, traffic accidents, and other health and social issues. According to USA Today article from a few years ago, federal health officials warned the public about a version of synthetic marijuana that was laced with rat poison. This mixture caused uncontrollable bleeding in hundreds of people and killed several others who inhaled it. There are ongoing stories about marijuana mixed with harmful chemicals.

Self-Care Tips that Will Change Your Life

You have more power than you think. This is an excellent time to practice self-care in a new way. As you continue growing, these self-care strategies will help you:

1. Get physical activity like walking, exercising, running, playing ball, or swimming.

2. Eat healthy foods and drink water.

3. Avoid drugs, and don't allow others to pressure you into experimenting or using them.

4. Practice good hygiene (such as bathing, brushing your teeth, and combing your hair).

5. Develop peaceful friendships and avoid stressful people.

6. Nurture your spirit by reflecting on your blessings and making time to do things that empower you.

SELF-CARE INVENTORY

1. What does your daily diet (food intake) look like?
_____
_____
_____

2. How many hours of sleep do you get?
_____
_____
_____

3. What physical activity are you doing? If none, what can you do?

_____

_____

_____

_____

4. Do you feel good about your hygiene? Is there anything you need so that you can take better care of your body? Let your parents, family, nurse, or counselor know if you need anything.

_____

_____

_____

_____

5 How can you improve your self-care?

_____

_____

_____

_____

6. Are you using your voice when it is necessary to protect yourself?

_____

_____

_____

Chapter 10: Love Your Wings

What Would You Do?

A couple of students in your class tease you because you have an underarm odor. Do you get mad at the students because they talk about your body odor? Or do you do the sniff test to see if there is odor so you can change your hygiene habits?

Remember this...

You deserve a hug and a pat on the back! Remember to show yourself some love and kindness. Take care of your beautiful body. Nourish it, feed it, and give it the sleep it needs. If you take care of your body, mind, and spirit, it will take care of you.

CHAPTER 11: MEASURE YOUR WINGSPAN — Evaluating Your Journey

Coach and Cathy gazed back their incredible journey and the strides they'd made. Cathy had acquired a wealth of knowledge about soaring through the skies and using her new wings. Coach cleared her throat and began, "Cathy, I'd like to talk about the concept of your wingspan. Your wingspan is the key to determining how high you will fly. Your wings have carried you to remarkable places.

The tools you were provided have been your guiding light on this transformational journey. Take a moment to honor your courage for attempting and embracing the art of flight. Think back to the beginning of this expedition when you were a humble caterpillar. Now, you've evolved as a beautiful butterfly!

Now is the perfect time to pause and reflect on the areas in which you've grown. Reflecting on your growth deepens your understanding of your potential. It's also a source of inspiration and self-confidence. You overcame obstacles and made magic throughout this incredible journey. I'm proud of you!"

Chapter 11: Measure Your Wingspan

Metamorphosis Map

Just as Cathy did, it's important for you to take a moment to think about your *wingspan*. That's a fancy way of saying how far you've come and how much you've grown. You've transformed and changed, just like she did. Now, let's consider all the places your wings carried you while following your metamorphosis map. This adventure was all about helping you become the best, most awesome version of yourself. And I truly believe you evolved into a better you.

Take a good look at the map below. See where you began and where you are now. Over time you will revisit the stops on this map.

Evaluate Your Growth

As you journeyed through this book and followed your metamorphosis map, you likely gained valuable insights about yourself. You might have discovered new ways to handle situations that once seemed challenging. By now, you grasp the significance of your mindset, habits, and values. It's time to evaluate your transformative experience and see just how much you've grown.

1. In which areas did you notice the most growth?
_____
_____
_____

2. In which areas do you feel you need to improve?
_____
_____
_____

Now, it's time to take a deeper look at your growth. Take a moment and complete the Metamorphosis Inventory on the next page.

Chapter 11: Measure Your Wingspan

MY METAMORPHOSIS EVALUATION

TOPICS COVERED	I learned something new	I noticed change and growth	No change
ATTITUDE	○	○	○
CONFIDENCE IN MYSELF	○	○	○
HABITS	○	○	○
HANDLING CONFLICT	○	○	○
CAREER KNOWLEDGE	○	○	○
FRIENDSHIPS	○	○	○
GIRL DRAMA	○	○	○
GOAL-SETTING	○	○	○
GRADES	○	○	○
LEADERSHIP	○	○	○
MANAGING MY EMOTIONS	○	○	○
MINDSET	○	○	○
PEER PRESSURE	○	○	○
TAKING RESPONSIBILITY	○	○	○
SELF-CARE (SLEEP, HEALTH, HYGIENE)	○	○	○
VALUING MYSELF	○	○	○

Keep Growing Your Wings

Reflecting on your personal growth is like reviewing a life report card! You'll find areas where you do well and others that need improvement. Remember, no one is perfect – we're all on a journey of learning and growth. You have the opportunity to strive towards being the best version of yourself.

If you've realized that your attitude could use some adjustment, take the initiative to work on it. If your habits hinder your success, it's within your power to change them. It's about committing to yourself to remain open to improvement. You've got this!

Remember to Use Your Tools

You've gathered many helpful tools to help you grow and succeed now. These tools aren't just for now; they'll also be super helpful as you evolve. They will also be helpful when you're all grown up. As you go through life, you'll face some difficult or uncomfortable situations, just like everyone else. Some of these situations might not be in your control, but you have total control over how you react to them. You can decide how you act and what you do. So, when things get tough, ask yourself, "How would an evolved girl handle this?

CHAPTER 12: BECOME A METAMORPHOSIS MENTOR — Inspire Change in Others

You've truly transformed into a remarkable young woman with beautiful wings! As an Evolved Girl, you have a special role and responsibility to help others on their journey. Here's how you can be a mentor and lead by example: share the wisdom you've gained, help guide others on their path to transformation, teach, support, and inspire someone. There are others out there who could use the same tools you've acquired. Make a positive impact in your unique way and help others grow their wings. This is what Evolved Girls do.

Who Can You Help?

Do you know someone who could use a little extra support? Maybe a classmate could use some cheering up or a sick grandparent could use your help. Perhaps you noticed that your teacher struggles in the morning carrying a big load of supplies and can use a hand. There are plenty of ways you can assist others on their journey.

You may have an opportunity to mentor or coach someone at your school. Do you remember how Coach guided Cathy on her journey to a metamorphosis? Coach was respectful, wise, and considerate of Cathy's feelings and circumstances. She never forced her opinion on Cathy.

There will be students, siblings, and friends that you will coach. There are students who look up to you. If you really want to help others experience transformation, express your interest to your parents and teacher. They may have ideas about how you can help others transform, just as Cathy did. The key idea here is to be a shining light for others, guiding them along the way.

Share Evolved Girl

You can help other girls evolve by sharing this book with them. Tell them about your experience. You can also tell your school principal or counselor about Evolved Girl and the Evolved Girl Empowerment Program. You can direct them to the website so that they can learn more – www.evolvedyou.net

Chapter 12: Become a Metamorphosis Mentor

METAMORPHOSIS MENTOR INVENTORY

1. Who needs encouragement or support in your classroom or school?
_____
_____
_____

2. Do you know someone in your family (sister or brother) who needs help or support that you are able to give?
_____
_____
_____

3. How can you use your superpowers, talent, and creativity to serve as an Evolved Girl Coach?
_____
_____
_____

Hi Evolved Girl!

I hope this book and our shared journey have sparked a transformation within you! I'm truly grateful that you invited me to be a part of this adventure with you. Never forget who you are! You are strong, beautiful, gifted, and one-of-a-kind.

I would love to hear how "Evolved Girl" has made a positive impact on your life. Feel free to share any ideas or feedback on how I can make the "Evolved Girl" experience even better.

Email: evolvedgirl@evolvedyou.net

To Your Evolution,

Dr. Jacqueline Deas

www.ingramcontent.com/pod-product-compliance
Lightning Source LLC
Chambersburg PA
CBHW050324010526
44119CB00003B/89